PASSPORT
TO
NARNIA

BOOKS BY GEORGE BEAHM

The Vaughn Bode Index ✍ *Kirk's Works: The Art of Tim Kirk* ✍*How to Sell Woodstoves* ✍ *How to Buy a Woodstove—and Not Get Burned* ✍ *Notes from Elam* (as editor) ✍ *Write to the Top* ✍ *The Stephen King Companion* ✍ *The Stephen King Story* ✍ *War of Words: The Censorship Debate* ✍ *Michael Jordan: Shooting Star* ✍ *The Stephen King Companion: Updated & Revised* ✍ *The Unauthorized Anne Rice Companion* ✍ *Stephen King: America's Best-Loved Boogeyman* ✍ *Stephen King from A to Z* ✍ *Stephen King Country* ✍ *Stephen King Collectibles* ✍ *The Patricia Cornwell Companion* ✍ *The Essential J. R. R. Tolkien Sourcebook* ✍ *How to Protect Yourself & Your Family Against Terrorism* ✍ *Muggles and Magic: An Unofficial Guide to J. K. Rowling and the Harry Potter Phenomenon* ✍ *Fact, Fiction, & Folklore in Harry Potter's World: An Unofficial Guide* ✍*Stephen King Collectibles: Updated & Revised* ✍ *Passport to Narnia: A Newcomer's Guide* ✍ *The Philip Pullman Companion: His Dark Materials.*

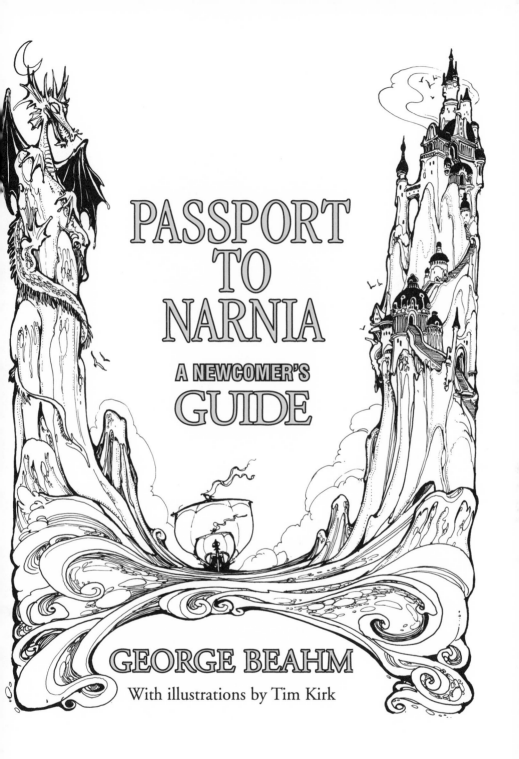

PASSPORT TO NARNIA

A NEWCOMER'S
GUIDE

GEORGE BEAHM

With illustrations by Tim Kirk

HAMPTON ROADS
PUBLISHING COMPANY, INC.

Disclaimer:
This book is not endorsed, approved, or authorized
by C. S. Lewis Private Limited, *HarperCollinsPublishers*, or The Walt Disney Company.

Cover design by Steve Amarillo
Cover images: wardrobe © Hemera Technologies Inc:, lamppost
and lion © Jupiter Images corporation. All rights reserved.

Hampton Roads Publishing Company, Inc.
1125 Stoney Ridge Road
Charlottesville, VA 22902 USA
434-296-2772
fax: 434-296-5096
e-mail: hrpc@hrpub.com
www.hrpub.com

If you are unable to order this book from your local bookseller,
you may order directly from the publisher. Call 1-800-766-8009.

Beahm, George W.
Passport to Narnia : a newcomer's guide / by George Beahm.
   p. cm.
Summary: "Passport to Narnia is a beginners guide to C.S. Lewis' classic
Chronicles of Narnia offering a book-by-book synopsis of the series, and an
in-depth look at the forthcoming movie series. Passport to Narnia also
includes a biography of Lewis, along with interviews, photos, a guide to C.
S. Lewis' England and more"--Provided by publisher.
   Includes bibliographical references.
   ISBN 1-57174-465-7 (alk. paper)
1. Lewis, C.S. (Clives Staples), 1898-1963. Chronicles of
Narnia--Handbooks, manuals, etc. 2. Children's stories, English--Handbooks,
manuals, etc. 3. Fantasy fiction, English--Handbooks, manuals, etc. 4.
Narnia (Imaginary place)--Handbooks, manuals, etc. I. Title.
   PR6023.E926C5316 2005.
   823'.912-dc22

                    20050279993

          ISBN 1-57174-465-7 (Trade Paperback)
          ISBN 1-57174-481-9 (Reinforced Library Binding)

          10 9 8 7 6 5 4 3 2 1
          Printed on acid-free paper in Canada

FOR HANNAH AND SETH

KIRK

If you become a writer you'll be trying to describe the thing all your life; and lucky if, out of dozens of books, one or two sentences, just for the moment, come near to getting it across.

❖ from C. S. Lewis in a 1956 letter to a boy named Martin (*C. S. Lewis Letters to Children*)

CONTENTS

A Short Note to the Reader

There are many books available about C. S. Lewis and, especially, Narnia, but most of them are scholarly or religious, so where is an introduction for new readers?

If you've found your way to Narnia through the Disney movie, this book will take you back through the wardrobe, as it were, and beyond. A primer on Lewis and his fictional world of Narnia, this book is intended to be a passport for new travelers.

Please note: If you are in a hurry to get to Narnia, go directly to part 2: The Books. But if you have the time to take a side trip first, proceed to part 1, so that you can understand a little about the man who created Narnia, which will explain a lot about the creation of Narnia itself.

Finally, after you've thoroughly explored this book, you can explore on your own in part 4, which gives my recommendations on other resources.

The wardrobe owned by C. S. Lewis now in the collection at the Marion E. Wade Center. (Used by permission of The Marion E. Wade Center, Wheaton College, Wheaton,
IL.)

INTRODUCTORY ESSAY
BY NEIL GAIMAN

I THOUGHT I'D TALK ABOUT AUTHORS, and about three authors in particular, and the circumstances in which I met them.

There are authors with whom one has a personal relationship and authors with whom one does not. There are the ones who change your life and the ones who don't. That's just the way of it.

I was six years old when I saw an episode of *The Lion, The Witch and the Wardrobe* in black and white on television at my grandmother's house in Portsmouth. I remember the beavers and the first appearance of Aslan, an actor in an unconvincing lion costume, standing on his hind legs, from which I deduce that this was probably episode two or three. I went home to Sussex and saved my meagre pocket money until I was able to buy a copy of *The Lion, The Witch and the Wardrobe* of my own. I read it, and *The Voyage of the Dawn Treader*, the other book I could find, over and over, and when my seventh birthday arrived I had dropped enough hints that my birthday present was a boxed set of the complete Narnia books. And I remember what I did on my seventh birthday—I lay on my bed and I read the books all through, from the first to the last.

For the next four or five years I continued to read them. I would read other books, of course, but in my heart I knew that I read them only because there weren't an infinite number of Narnia books to read.

For good or ill, the religious allegory, such as it was, went entirely over my head, and it was not until I was about twelve that I found myself realising that there were Certain Parallels. Most people get it at the Stone Table; I got it when it suddenly occurred to me that the story of the events that occurred to Saint Paul on the road to Damascus was the dragoning of Eustace Scrubb all over again. I was personally offended: I felt that an author, whom I had trusted, had had a hidden agenda. I had nothing against religion, or religion in fiction—I had bought (in the school bookshop) and loved *The Screwtape Letters*, and was already dedicated to G. K. Chesterton. My upset was, I think, that it made less of Narnia for me, it made it less interesting a thing, less interesting a place. Still, the lessons of Narnia sank deep. Aslan telling the Tash worshippers that the prayers they had given to Tash were actually prayers to Him was something I believed then, and ultimately still believe.

The Pauline Baynes map of Narnia poster stayed up on my bedroom wall through my teenage years.

I didn't return to Narnia until I was a parent, first in 1988, then in 1999, each time reading all the books aloud to my children. I found that the things that I loved, I still loved—sometimes loved more—while the things that I had thought odd as a child (the awkwardness of the structure of *Prince Caspian*, and my dislike for most of *The Last Battle*, for example) had intensified; there were also some new things that made me really uncomfortable— for example the role of women in the Narnia books, culminating in the disposition of Susan. But what I found more interesting was how much of the Narnia books had crept inside me: as I would write there would be moment after moment of realising that I'd borrowed phrases, rhythms, the way that words were put together; for example, that I had a hedgehog and a hare, in *The Books of Magic*, speaking and agreeing with each other much as the Dufflepuds do.

C. S. Lewis was the first person to make me want to be a writer. He made me aware of the writer, that there was someone standing behind the words, that there was someone telling the story. I fell in love with the way he used parentheses—the auctorial asides that were both wise and chatty, and I rejoiced in using such brackets in my own essays and compositions through the rest of my childhood. I think, perhaps, the genius of Lewis was that he made a world that was more real to me than the one I lived in; and if authors got to write the tales of Narnia, then I wanted to be an author.

Now, if there is a wrong way to find Tolkien, I found Tolkien entirely the wrong way. Someone had left a copy of a paperback called *The Tolkien Reader* in my house. It contained an essay "Tolkien's Magic Ring" by Peter S. Beagle—some poetry, *Leaf By Niggle* and *Farmer Giles of Ham*. In retrospect, I suspect I picked it up only because it was illustrated by Pauline Baynes. I would have been eight, maybe nine years old.

What was important to me, reading that book, was the poetry, and the promise of a story.

Now, when I was nine I changed schools, and I found, in the class library, a battered and extremely elderly copy of *The Hobbit*. I bought it from the school in a library sale for a penny, along with an ancient copy of the *Plays of W. S. Gilbert*, and I still have it.

It would be another year or so before I was to discover the first two volumes of *The Lord of the Rings* in the main school library. I read them. I read them over and over: I would finish *The*

Two Towers and start again at the beginning of *The Fellowship of the Ring*. I never got to the end. This was not the hardship it may sound—I had already learned from the Peter S. Beagle essay in the *Tolkien Reader* that it would all come out more or less okay. Still, I really did want to read it for myself.

When I was thirteen I won the school English Prize, and was allowed to choose a book. I chose *The Return of the King*. I still own it. I only read it once, however—thrilled to find out how the story ended—because around the same time I also bought the one-volume paperback edition. It was the most expensive thing I had bought with my own money, and it was that which I now read and reread.

I came to the conclusion that *The Lord of the Rings* was, most probably, the best book that ever could be written, which put me in something of a quandary. I wanted to be a writer when I grew up. (That's not true: I wanted to be a writer then.) And I wanted to write *The Lord of the Rings*. The problem was that it had already been written.

I gave the matter a great deal of thought, and eventually came to the conclusion that the best thing would be if, while holding a copy of *The Lord of the Rings*, I slipped into a parallel universe in which Professor Tolkien had not existed. And then I would get someone to retype the book—I knew that if I sent a publisher a book that had already been published, even in a parallel universe, they'd get suspicious, just as I knew my own thirteen-year-old typing skills were not going to be up to the job of typing it. And once the book was published I would, in this parallel universe, be the author of *Lord of the Rings*, than which there can be no better thing. And I read *Lord of the Rings* until I no longer needed to read it, because it was inside me. Years later, I dropped Christopher Tolkien a letter, explaining something that he found himself unable to footnote, and was profoundly gratified to find myself thanked in the Tolkien book *The Return of the Shadow* (for something I had learned from reading James Branch Cabell, no less).

It was in the same school library that had the two volumes of *Lord of the Rings* that I discovered Chesterton. The library was next door to the school matron's office, and I learned that, when faced with lessons that I disliked from teachers who terrified me, I could always go up to the matron's office and plead a headache. A bitter-tasting aspirin would be dissolved in a glass of water, I would drink it down, trying not to make a face, and then be sent to sit in the library while I waited for it to work. The library was also where I went on wet afternoons, and whenever else I could.

The first Chesterton book I found there was *The Complete Father Brown Stories*. There were hundreds of other authors I encountered in that library for the first time—Edgar Wallace and Baroness Orczy and Dennis Wheatley and the rest of them. But Chesterton was important—as important to me in his way as C. S. Lewis had been.

You see, while I loved Tolkien and while I wished to have written his book, I had no desire at all to write like him. Tolkien's words and sentences seemed like natural things, like rock formations or waterfalls, and wanting to write like Tolkien would have been, for me, like wanting to blossom like a cherry tree or climb a tree like a squirrel or rain like a thunderstorm. Chesterton was the complete opposite. I was always aware, reading Chesterton, that there was someone writing this who rejoiced in words, who deployed them on the page as an artist deploys his paints upon his palette. Behind every Chesterton sentence there was someone painting with words, and it seemed to me that at the end of any particularly good sentence or any perfectly put paradox, you could hear the author, somewhere behind the scenes, giggling with delight.

Father Brown, that prince of humanity and empathy, was a gateway drug into the harder stuff, this being a one-volume collection of three novels: *The Napoleon of Notting Hill* (my favourite piece of predictive 1984 fiction, and one that hugely informed my own novel *Neverwhere*), *The Man Who Was Thursday* (the prototype of all twentieth century spy stories, as well as being a Nightmare, and a theological delight), and lastly *The Flying Inn* (which had some excellent poetry in it, but which struck me, as an eleven-year-old, as being oddly small-minded; I suspected that Father Brown would have found it so as well). Then there were the poems and the essays and the art.

Chesterton and Tolkien and Lewis were, as I've said, not the only writers I read between the ages of six and thirteen, but they were the authors I read over and over again; each of them played a part in building me. Without them, I cannot imagine that I would have become a writer, and certainly not a writer of fantastic fiction. I would not have understood that the best way to show people true things is from a direction that they had not imagined the truth coming, nor that the majesty and the magic of belief and dreams could be a vital part of life and of writing.

And without those three writers, I would not be here today. And nor, of course, would any of you.

I thank you.

Neil Gaiman delivered this speech to members of the Mythopoeic Society at Mythcon 35.

PREFACE
BY GEORGE BEAHM

No book is really worth reading at the age of ten which is not equally (and often far more) worth reading at the age of fifty. . . . The only imaginative works we ought to grow out of are those which it would have been better not to have read at all.

❖C. S. Lewis on children's books,
"On Stories" in *Of Other Worlds: Essays and Stories*

FOR OVER A HALF CENTURY, *The Lord of the Rings* has won a place not only on bookshelves around the world but in the hearts of millions of readers when they want to escape from our world to find refuge and solace in Tolkien's fictional world of Middle-earth.

Until recently, the only passports to Middle-earth were the original text or a film adaptation in 1978 by Ralph Bakshi.

That changed in 2001 when New Zealand filmmaker Peter Jackson literally put New Zealand on the map, with the result that New Zealand is now Middle-earth in the minds of millions: a notion that New Zealand's tourist industry actively promotes. New Zealand, according to its tourism bureau, *is* Middle-earth— or so they would like you to believe. In truth, New Zealand is where Peter Jackson *filmed* his adaptation of Professor Tolkien's *The Lord of the Rings* and where (if Jackson is once again at the helm) *The Hobbit* will be filmed.

Middle-earth, which was for many years only a literary destination, became a world destination. New Zealand, overrun by hobbits, orcs, wizards, elves, and the race of men from its Third Age during the back-to-back filming of the movie, found itself on the map as a favorite tourist destination when moviegoers and readers showed up en masse to experience Middle-earth, or at least its closest geographic approximation.

The same phenomenon happened when J. K. Rowling's fictional world of Harry Potter, brought visually to life by directors Chris Columbus and Alfonso Cuarón, was filmed in Scotland and England. Those film adaptations prompted moviegoers and readers to experience firsthand the Muggle world of Harry Potter and his wizarding world (or at least its movie equivalent).

Likewise, Narnia should brace itself for the arrival of tourists, for they will soon be coming in droves.

Since the publication of Lewis's first book in the series, *The Lion, the Witch and the Wardrobe* in 1950, Narnia has been, and continues to be, the favorite destination of his fans, especially his younger ones. But armchair travelers will take a giant step forward with the December 9, 2005 release of *The Chronicles of Narnia: The Lion, the Witch and the Wardrobe* from Disney.

What the newcomers to Narnia will soon discover is that, unlike Tolkien's *The Lord of the Rings*, which was made into three movies (one for each book), the Chronicles of Narnia are comprised of seven interrelated novels, and—should the series prove popular—there's the possibility that original movies will be made, since Hollywood contracts typically reserve that right.

For good reason, Disney is using the tagline, "There are a thousand stories about Narnia. This is one of them."

Although Lewis was adamant that there would only be seven books about Narnia, Disney executives would love to see film adaptations of the Chronicles go on forever, or at least until the "property" (an ugly word!) loses its box office luster.

Should Disney go that route—film beyond the seven original novels by adding sequels—I shouldn't think that people familiar with Hollywood's practices would be surprised; however, they might be disappointed, since the curse of "sequelitis," from *Star Wars* to *The Terminator*, has proven to be the death knell of virtually every film franchise. The closest analogy I can think of in Narnian terms is the dying world of Charn, chronicled in *The Magician's Nephew*, in which an evil queen speaks the Deplorable Word, and thereby dooms, and damns, her world and every living thing in it, including herself.

At the heart of any good work of fiction is story, and story is what Tolkien's *The Lord of the Rings* is all about; likewise, story is what Lewis's Chronicles of Narnia is all about, as well.

As with Tolkien, Lewis and his works have achieved a mythic status, to the point where British author Philip Pullman took Lewis, and, specifically, the Chronicles of Narnia, to task for what he perceived as literary sins, both of commission and omission.

Pullman, best known for the three books that comprise the His Dark Materials series, is rightly hailed as one of the world's most imaginative and, as is obvious to anyone who has read those three novels, audacious writers today. But clearly there are millions who feel differently, for Narnia not only has stood the test of time but of numbers as well, with an astonishing 85 million copies of the Chronicles of Narnia sold worldwide in thirty languages.

The din of voices, as if it weren't loud enough already, will become increasingly louder as C. S. Lewis (or Jack, as he preferred to call himself) takes center stage, not only in the movie theaters worldwide but in bookstores, where shelves already groan under the weight of books by and about him.

There's no doubt about it: Jack is back.

Biographies, concordances, quote books, encyclopedias—you name it, and it's likely already available. And, if not, you'll see more soon enough. Hoping for a successful franchise on the order of *The Lord of the Rings*, Disney and its publishing partners will be issuing dozens of tie-in editions to bookstores, just in time for the film's release on December 9, 2005.

The newcomer will understandably be confused by the bewildering array of books not only by Lewis but also about him. Appealing to students, scholars, devout Christians, and lay readers, Lewis has been endlessly chronicled, but most of these books presume you are already familiar with Lewis and his works and give you more of the same.

Keeping that perspective in mind, I wanted to write an accessible guide. This book, I hope, will be your passport to Narnia. We'll soon go into the room where the enchanted wardrobe awaits us, but before we do, we must go next door to visit the man who conceived of Narnia.

No pushing, no shoving, and do have your passports ready, so come this way. . . .

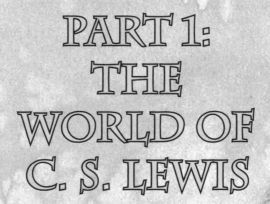

PART 1:
THE
WORLD OF
C. S. LEWIS

C. S. Lewis:
An Abbreviated Chronology

November 29, 1898: Clive Staples Lewis born in Belfast, Ireland.

1905: The Lewis family moves to Little Lea near Belfast.

August 23, 1908: His mother, Flora Lewis, dies of cancer.

August 4, 1914: The beginning of World War I.

September 19, 1914: Lewis studies privately with William T. Kirkpatrick, who is the inspiration for the Professor in *The Lion, the Witch and the Wardrobe*.

April–September 1916: Lewis attends University College, Oxford.

November 1917: Lewis goes off to the front lines as a second lieutenant in the infantry to fight in the war.

November 11, 1918: World War I ends.

1919: Lewis resumes studies at University College, graduating in 1923.

May 20, 1925: Lewis begins teaching at Magdalen College, Oxford.

October 1930: Lewis purchases (with his brother and Mrs. Moore) a home near Oxford, named The Kilns.

September 2, 1939: London evacuees (children) come to The Kilns.

1950: Publication of *The Lion, the Witch and the Wardrobe* (the first book in the series of the Chronicles of Narnia).

1951: Publication of *Prince Caspian*.

1952: Publication of *The Voyage of the* Dawn Treader. Lewis meets his wife-to-be, Helen Joy Davidman, whom he had met through correspondence two years earlier.

1953: Publication of *The Silver Chair*.

1954: Publication of *The Horse and His Boy*.

1955: Publication of *The Magician's Nephew*.

1956: Publication of *The Last Battle*; Lewis receives the Carnegie Medal for it. April 23, Lewis marries Helen Joy Davidman in a civil ceremony.

July 13, 1960: Lewis's wife dies (cause: cancer).

November 22, 1963: C. S. Lewis dies (age 64).

1971: Lewis's stepsons sell the copyright to Lewis's works to C. S. Lewis Private Limited.

December 9, 2005: The first major motion picture from the Chronicles of Narnia to be released, an adaptation of *The Lion, the Witch and the Wardrobe*, by Disney Pictures.

C. S. Lewis:
The Man behind
the Magic of Narnia

It is never safe to attribute a man's imaginations too directly to
his experience.

❖C. S. Lewis,
English Literature in the Sixteenth Century

The antique wardrobe at the Marion E. Wade Center in
Wheaton, Illinois, stands seven feet high and four feet wide. A
nearby plaque reads: "Enter at your own risk. The Wade Center
assumes no responsibility for persons who disappear or who are
lost in this wardrobe."

It is arguably the most famous wardrobe in literary history,
for it belonged to the grandfather of Lewis; and when Lewis was

a small boy, living at Little Lea near Belfast, Ireland, his brother and one of his cousins would sit in this very wardrobe as he held their rapt attention by spinning tales.

Was there some magic in that wardrobe after all? Or perhaps the magic was mostly in the storyteller—but the storyteller is gone. What's left are the stories and the wardrobe that, along with other Lewis holdings, is part of the permanent collection at the Wade Center, which is the repository for a treasure trove of Lewis material. In any case, the visitors to the Wade Center are amazed to see the wealth of material on hand, ranging from personal letters, manuscripts, books from his library, books about him, photos, and memorabilia, including a writing desk and a fountain pen.

The magic began on November 29, 1898, when Albert J. Lewis and his wife, Flora, added a second son, Clive Staples Lewis, to the family (their first son, Warren Hamilton Lewis, had been born three years earlier).

But, at an early age, Clive Staples Lewis decided he wanted to be called "Jacksie" and told his mother so. Not surprisingly, she humored him, thinking it was a child at play, a mere fancy, but she was surprised when he would later only answer to "Jack."

From that time on, he was known to family and friends as Jack Lewis, the name he preferred over his given name.

Growing up in Strandtown near Belfast, Ireland, at the Leeborough House, which the family called Little Lea, the Lewis brothers frequently found themselves indoors during inclement weather. The conventional wisdom back then was that children could catch tuberculosis during periods of heavy rain. And since Ireland is famous for its rain, especially in the winter, confinement indoors was a way of life.

Back then, there were no televisions, no computers, no cellular phones, no electronic games, and no DVDs. In other words, no passive forms of entertainment. Actively engaging his imagination, Lewis showed a dual talent not only for drawing—a discipline he never pursued—but also for writing, which early on he pursued with zeal. With his brother, C. S. Lewis invented Boxen, a land of talking animals.

This was a happy time for the boys, a time of innocence. But in 1908, innocence turned into experience: their idyllic world turned bleak when their mother died in her mid-forties.

The boys' lives were understandably shattered and, increasingly, each boy put his faith in the other. As C. S. Lewis would later write in *Surprised by Joy*, they were "two frightened urchins huddled for warmth in a bleak world."

The experience of watching his mother's slow decline from health to sickness would later find expression in *The Magician's Nephew*, in which Digory Kirke would appeal to Aslan to help save his dying mother. With Aslan's permission, Digory plucks an apple from the Tree in Narnia and brings it back to his world, where he cuts it up in pieces and feeds it to his dying mother, who undergoes a miraculous transformation from sickness to health.

Soon after their mother's death, the Lewis boys left Little Lea behind and entered the public school system. Going from school to school, C. S. Lewis was never happy until, at fourteen, he was placed under the tutelage of William T. Kirkpatrick. Lewis studied under Kirkpatrick for three blissful years. Years later, Kirkpatrick would appear as Professor Digory Kirke in the first published Narnia book, *The Lion, the Witch and the Wardrobe*. Intellectually rigorous, Kirkpatrick found an eager and willing student in Lewis, who affectionately termed him "The Great Knock" because of the impact of his logical thinking.

In 1916, Lewis studied at University College, but his studies were interrupted—as was the case for so many others, including J. R. R. Tolkien—by World War I, known as the Great War, and also the War to End All Wars.

Lewis went to the front lines in 1917, where he was wounded

in battle the following year; he was sent to recuperate in a hospital. The Great War ended on November 11, 1918, and Lewis resumed his studies. He excelled in Greek and Latin literature, philosophy, ancient history, and English.

After teaching philosophy for one year at University College, Lewis began teaching in 1925 at Magdalen College, Oxford, where he would remain for nearly three decades.

The following year, he met J. R. R. Tolkien, who had come from Leeds University. For nearly four decades, they shared a symbiotic relationship, both personal and professional: Tolkien, a philologist, was a worldbuilder whose stories of Middle-earth found a ready audience in Lewis, who recognized their literary merits. Of Lewis, Tolkien observed that without his encouragement, *The Lord of the Rings* might never have been written.

Tolkien influenced Lewis as well. Having abandoned Christianity as a young teenager, Lewis, an atheist, embraced it once more after a long discussion with Tolkien and H. V. D. Dyson about the storytelling and mythmaking in the Bible.

Lewis would go on to become one of the world's most popular Christian writers, publishing major works of nonfiction empowered by his renewed faith. Similarly, the power found in his most popular fiction, the Chronicles of Narnia, is inextricably linked to elements of religious symbolism that would likely be absent if Lewis had not met Tolkien.

On September 1, 1939, when Germany invaded Poland, both the British and the French declared war on Germany, marking the start of World War II. In the next week, not only would C. S. Lewis's brother Warren be recalled to active duty, but their home, The Kilns (named after its brick kilns) would serve as a rural refuge for children from London—an estimated 1.5 million dispersed in just a few days.

It was from one of these evacuees, a young girl who wondered what was behind the wardrobe in his house, that Lewis got the idea of writing a novel centered on four children whose circumstances were similar: forced to leave London for the countryside to live with an older man.

That eventually became the basic storyline for *The Lion, the Witch and the Wardrobe*, but the enchanted wardrobe would remain closed for another decade: Narnia had not yet fully formed in Lewis's mind.

Just as Tolkien had read his fiction to Lewis, who saw in it the work of genius, Lewis had hoped for a similar sympathy from Tolkien for his own fiction about Narnia. Unfortunately, Tolkien, who had an active distaste for allegory in fiction, felt the religious aspects were too obvious and famously remarked, "It is sad that 'Narnia' and all that part of C. S. L.'s work should remain outside the range of my sympathy."

In a foreword to *The Lord of the Rings*, Tolkien made his opinion clear: "I cordially dislike allegory in all its manifestations, and always have done since I grew old and wary enough to detect its presence."

Fortunately, a mutual friend Roger Lancelyn Green, who was also a member of the informal literary group that included both writers (and others), felt just as strongly that Lewis had written a wonderful book—a classic, in fact.

In this instance, Tolkien's assessment missed the mark, but Green's hit it dead-on. The Narnian Chronicles would prove to be Lewis's most popular work.

As it sometimes happens, the story itself imposed its own will on the storyteller. In Lewis's case, the pivotal element was the unexpected arrival of Aslan bounding in, making a dramatic appearance that fundamentally changed the tone of the first book and the remaining six as well. Indeed, Aslan is the only major figure that appears in all seven of the books that comprise the Chronicles of Narnia.

A lifelong bachelor, C. S. Lewis, at age fifty-one, found his world forever changed when Helen Joy Davidman entered his life. In January 1950, she had written a letter to him. She subsequently came to Oxford to meet Lewis, bringing along her two sons, Douglas and David. Her first marriage was over, and the divorce was only a matter of time.

Unbidden and unforeseen, the friendship blossomed into love, and six years after that initial letter, the two were married on April 1956.

Lewis and Davidman both found late in life a joy in each other that had long eluded both of them—a marriage of minds. The marriage, however, was not destined to last: Davidman was diagnosed with terminal cancer—an echo of what Lewis went through with his mother.

Helen, who had finally met and married her soul mate, had scant time to come home to The Kilns and enjoy their remaining time together.

In 1960, Helen finally succumbed, leaving behind her two sons and a grieving husband who, for a few brief years, had known a kind of transcendent happiness that had previously eluded him in life. Lewis never came to terms with the loss.

Three years later, on November 22, Lewis himself died; the day was also marked by the passing of Aldous Huxley and the death of President John F. Kennedy. On that day, Camelot—fictionalized in Lewis's Narnian Chronicles and idealized in Kennedy's administration—became history.

Warren Lewis survived his brother by another decade, but he finally passed on in 1973.

The two brothers were buried at a grave site in Headington Quarry, Oxford, on the grounds of Holy Trinity Church.

Under the terms of Lewis's will, he fulfilled a promise to his wife: her sons would inherit the literary estate; they would jointly own the keys to Narnia and all that it contained.

In July 1998, the Mythopoeic Society celebrated at Wheaton College the centenary of Lewis's birth. Honoring his considerable literary achievements—from the Christian writings for lay readers to the novels, including the Chronicles of Narnia and his other imaginative fiction—the members of the international group raised their glasses in a heartfelt salute to Clive Staples Lewis, who opened the way to Narnia so that the rest of us could eagerly follow.

The Real World of C. S. Lewis: His Main Haunts

To UNDERSTAND AND APPRECIATE Lewis and his work, it helps to know the geographical places that marked his life.

A detailed place-by-place look at all of his haunts—personal and professional—is beyond the scope of this book; for more information, consult the standards on the subject, notably *Touring C. S. Lewis' Ireland & England* (Perry C. Bramlett and Ronald W. Higdon), and *A Guide to the C. S. Lewis Tour in Oxford* (Ron Brind).

Ireland

Most people rightly associate Lewis with Oxford and Cambridge, since both are inextricably linked to his professional career as a professor and writer. Still, to overlook his native Ireland is a mistake, for it is Ireland where he was born and grew up, and which gave him some of his most cherished memories.

Belfast is where Lewis was born. Located in the eastern part of the city, in an area known as Strandtown, his home was located on Dundela Avenue. Unfortunately, the house no longer exists; it was leveled to make way for apartments.

Little Lea, the childhood home of Lewis, stills stands and has a placard outside marking it as his residence from 1905 to 1917. The house can be found at 76 Circular Road. This is where he first encountered his grandfather's wardrobe, which is now part of the permanent collection of Lewis memorabilia at Wheaton College in Wheaton, Illinois.

Of particular interest to C. S. Lewis fans: Little Lea had a small end room, which is where he and his brother, Warren, enjoyed creating new worlds, drawing and writing about Boxen, a medieval land of talking animals. In his autobiography, *Surprised by Joy*, Lewis wrote: "The Animal-Land . . . was a modern Animal-Land; it had to have trains and steamships. . . ."

Also of interest: William T. Kirkpatrick, an early tutor and a big influence on Lewis, lived in a house near the center of Belfast, on 21 Eliza Street. Kirkpatrick was the model for Professor Digory Kirke (a character from *The Lion, the Witch and the Wardrobe* and *The Magician's Nephew*). Lewis nicknamed Kirkpatrick "The Great Knock," an affectionate term he coined because of Kirkpatrick's logical mind, and the impact that kind of thinking had on Lewis as a young and impressionable boy who was looking for answers and found them in Kirkpatrick's rigorous, intellectual approach.

England

Oxford University is comprised of forty-six colleges. For anyone with more than a casual interest in contemporary fantasy, a visit to Oxford University is a must. Not only did C. S. Lewis teach here, but so did J. R. R. Tolkien. Among today's writers, J. K. Rowling applied but failed to gain entrance, though ironically its Christ Church College became a popular tourist destination after being featured prominently as a location for the film adaptations of her Harry Potter novels. Also, Philip Pullman, who is considered by many to be among the most imaginative British writers, graduated from and subsequently taught at Oxford; moreover, his fictional Oxford, depicted in the His Dark Materials trilogy, is the backdrop for one of the most engaging characters in recent memory, a spunky young girl named Lyra Belacqua.

Lewis's connections to Oxford are extensive, since it is here that he spent the bulk of his professional career, making a name for himself as a distinguished lecturer, critic, writer, and (to J. R. R. Tolkien's distress) a popularizer of the Christian faith.

Lewis taught at Magdalen College, which made a deep initial impression on him. In a 1925 letter to his father after arriving on campus, C. S. Lewis wrote, "My external surroundings are beautiful beyond expectation and beyond hope."

Some years later, in 1931, it was here that after a long walk and talk into the night, J. R. R. Tolkien and H. V. D. Dyson convinced C. S. Lewis to abandon his long-held views of atheism for Christianity.

Years later, in *Mere Christianity*, a collection of popular radio broadcasts published in book form in 1952, he explained the unanswered concerns about atheism that led him to question his lack of faith. "Thus in the very act of trying to prove that God did not exist—in other words, that the whole of reality was senseless—I found I was forced to assume that one part of reality . . . was full of sense. Consequently atheism turns out to be too simple. If the whole universe has no meaning, we should never have found out that it has no meaning."

Magdalen College (Oxford). Late in life, in 1954, Lewis left Oxford's Magdalen College (where he had taught for nearly three decades) to spend his final years as a scholar at Magdalene College in Cambridge. Although he gave lectures, he wasn't burdened with time-consuming tutorials, as indicated on the Web site of Mansfield College (Oxford University):

> At Oxford, the essential instrument of teaching is the tutorial system rather than lectures, classroom discussions, or seminars. The tutorial requires a great deal of self-motivation on the part of the student, as well as considerable independent organization and basic research skills. At the tutorial, the student reads a prepared paper on a topic assigned by the tutor; the student's paper, attendant readings, and research are the basis of a further discussion of the area under study.

The Bodleian Library is one of two major repositories of C. S. Lewis papers (the other is the Wade Center at Wheaton College, Illinois). With an excellent collection of letters, manuscripts, principal and secondary works, the Bodleian is not a lending library, and only those with a university affiliation or university sponsorship are allowed to access its considerable holdings.

The Eagle and Child (also known as the Bird and Baby) on Woodstock Road in Oxford. Perhaps best known as the meeting place of the Inklings, an informal group of learned friends that included C. S. and W. H. Lewis, J. R. R. Tolkien, H. V. D. Dyson, Charles Williams, and, occasionally, Owen Barfield, among others. Its back room ("the Rabbit Room") hosted their meetings. It was here that Tolkien read from his works in progress—including the early drafts of *The Lord of the Rings*, which Lewis termed the "new Hobbit." Lewis also read to the group from his nonfiction books.

A plaque on the premises marks its rich literary history: "C. S. Lewis, his brother W. H. Lewis, J. R. R. Tolkien, Charles Williams and other friends met every Tuesday morning, between the years 1939–1962 in the back room of this, their favourite pub. These men, popularly known as 'The Inklings,' met here to drink beer and to discuss, among other things, the books they were writing."

Every lover of fantasy should go to this famous pub and raise a pint of ale and toast the memories of all these fine gentlemen.

The Kilns is a must-see for any Lewis fan. Named after the kilns on the premises, used to fire bricks in earlier days, The Kilns was bought by C. S. Lewis, his brother, and Mrs. Janie King Moore, who moved in with her daughter, Maureen, in 1930. (Mrs. Moore's son, a fellow officer and friend of C. S. Lewis, was killed during World War I; Lewis fulfilled a promise to take care of his friend's mother.)

The Kilns was where Helen Joy Davidman and C. S. Lewis were married in a bedside ceremony in 1957. On November 22, 1963, one week before his birthday, C. S. Lewis passed away there.

The Kilns is now owned by the C. S. Lewis Foundation, which uses it principally as an academic retreat, under the auspices of the C. S. Lewis Foundation Study Centre.

> Through its English counterpart, The Kilns (Oxford) Limited, the Foundation has acquired and maintains The Kilns, C. S. Lewis' former home in Oxford. Since 1993, hundreds from America and Britain, all lovers of C. S. Lewis, have labored to restore and furnish the home as a Christian study centre. To the greater glory of God, the restoration was completed in 2001, and The Kilns was dedicated in July 2002 to its purpose as a focal point of Christian hospitality, study, reflection and learned conversation between Christian scholars, artists, and laity the world over.
>
> The C. S. Lewis Study Centre at The Kilns began with its Summer Seminars-in-Residence program in 2001 and has continued and expanded each summer since then. A maximum of eight participants each week enjoy the intimate seminar setting at The Kilns with a Lewis scholar in residence.

Holy Trinity Church (Headington Quarry, Oxford) is nearby The Kilns, approximately a mile away. Is is here that C. S. Lewis, along with his brother, was laid to rest, their grave sites marked by a single marble stone.

The Narnia Lamppost (in Grantchester, south of Cambridge). A student of Lewis's, Dr. M. A. Manzalaoui believes that in the town of Grantchester, Lewis found the inspiration for the lamppost now made famous by *The Lion, the Witch and the Wardrobe*. Located in a clearing in a field, the lamppost was used to illuminate the area. Wouldn't it be fun to think his theory to be true?

PART 2:
THE BOOKS

EDITH NESBIT, C. S. LEWIS, AND NARNIA

And it was then that she saw the extraordinary name "Whereveryou-wanttogoto." This was odd—but the name of the station from which it started was still more extraordinary, for it was not Euston or Cannon Street or Marylebone.

The name of the station was "Bigwardrobeinspareroom." And below this name, really quite unusual for a station, Amabel read in small letters:

"Single fares strictly forbidden. Return tickets No Class Nuppence. Trains leave Bigwardrobeinspareroom all the time."

❖ from "The Aunt and Amabel" by Edith Nesbit,
published in *Blackie's Christmas Annual* (1908)

ONCE UPON A TIME there were a group of children who moved from London to the countryside, where they discovered a passageway to another world and also met many strange but interesting talking creatures in the process.

Sounds like Lewis's Narnia books, doesn't it?

Actually, it's the work of a British woman named Edith Nesbit, who was a well-known and popular turn-of-the-century writer whom Lewis read when he was a child.

Edith Nesbit published, all told, sixty books for children, including twenty collaborations. From www.answers.com:

> According to her biographer Julia Briggs, Nesbit was "the first modern writer for children": Nesbit helped to reverse the great tradition of children's literature inaugurated by Carroll, MacDonald and Kenneth Grahame, in turning away from their secondary worlds to the tough truths to be won from encounters with things-as-they are, previously the province of adult novels.

Briggs also credits Nesbit with having invented the children's adventure story. Nesbit also popularized an innovative style of children's fantasy that combined realistic, contemporary children in real-world settings with magical objects and adventures.

Lewis scholar Kathryn Lindskoog points out several instances of inspiration that Lewis found in Nesbit's books:

In Nesbit's *The Story of the Amulet*, the children accidentally bring back to London an ancient Babylonian queen who goes on the rampage. In Lewis's *The Magician's Nephew*, the children accidentally bring back to London from Charn an ancient queen who goes on the rampage.

In Nesbit's novel, the first line of the book reads: "There were once four children . . . whose names were Cyril, Robert, Anthea and Jane. . . ." In *The Lion, the Witch and the Wardrobe*, the first line reads: "Once there were four children whose names were Peter, Susan, Edmund and Lucy." (For more linkages to Lewis's fiction, consult Lindskoog's *Journey into Narnia*).

For readers who want a taste of what Lewis read when he was a child, Nesbit's trilogy—*Railway Children*, *The Phoenix and the Carpet*, and *The Story of the Amulet*—is a good place to start. As all of these are in the public domain, e-books are freely available on the World Wide Web.

"I'll see you back to the lamppost. I suppose you can find your own way from there back to Spare Oom and War Drobe?"
❖Mr. Tumnus the faun, talking to Lucy Pevensie,
in *The Lion, the Witch and the Wardrobe*.

NARNIA:
A PUBLISHING FRANCHISE

Fifty-five years ago, with the publication of *The Lion, the Witch and the Wardrobe*, C. S. "Jack" Lewis opened the way to Narnia for the rest of the world. Since that time, 85 million copies of that book and the other six that comprise the Chronicles of Narnia have sold worldwide in thirty languages. It is an impressive achievement that speaks of the enduring popularity of the series, which has been discovered by each passing generation.

Today's Narnian devotees are fortunate because they can buy all seven novels at once, whereas the original audience had to read them one year apart, starting in 1950, until the final book (*The Last Battle*) saw publication in 1956.

Unlike our time, when popular books are commonly available in multiple formats (limited editions, trade editions in hardback and paperback, audiobooks on cassette and CD, dramatizations, and electronic books), back then the choice was made for you: buy the hardback edition—or do without. Given that fact, the series' sales record is all the more impressive. What, one wonders, would the sales of the Chronicles have been if multiple—and cheaper—editions had been available?

With the release of the film adaptation of *The Lion, the Witch and the Wardrobe* on December 9, 2005, moviegoers who discover the world beyond the wardrobe will head to bookstores to find a bewildering array of books by and about Lewis available in every possible edition. Novice Lewis readers will understandably be confused, since they are likely to be principally interested in obtaining all seven books in the series and, perhaps, a secondary book (or two) to serve as a roadmap for further excursions into Narnia or the world of Lewis.

It's not surprising that Walt Disney Pictures passed on *The Lord of the Rings*, since the scope of the story and the special effects required made the project a financial risk, aggravated by the fact that severe compression would be required to translate the story to film—if, indeed, it could be done without severely affecting the film. That Disney's track record with fantasy—notably *The Dark Crystal*—was disappointing, meant that little support among its executives could be garnered for *The Lord of the Rings*. So, not surprisingly, when Miramax attempted to sell its parent company on a three-film project with a $300 million budget, Disney not only balked but also choked. In typical fashion, Disney sought to cut costs by suggesting that the three films be compressed to two films—an absurd suggestion director Peter Jackson dismissed outright.

After Disney passed, New Line Cinema picked up the project and put its faith in Peter Jackson, and the film went on to become not only a critical success but a financial one. In fact, on Oscar night *The Return of the King* won in every category in which it was nominated—the *only* film in the history of the Academy Awards to have done so!

Fantasy, finally, had arrived, as director Steven Spielberg told Sean Astin (Samwise Gamgee from *The Lord of the Rings*), who agreed with Spielberg that fantasy films now enjoyed the respectability that had long eluded the genre.

As a result, Hollywood began actively seeking to duplicate the success of *The Lord of the Rings* by buying up other well-known fantasy books, including (you guessed it) The Chronicles of Narnia.

Disney, hoping to build a film and merchandising franchise around Narnia, is sparing no expense. Hiring Weta Workshop—the New Zealand company that did the costuming and special effects for *The Lord of the Rings*—and investing an estimated $150 million with its partner Walden Media, Disney's investment may pay off, and in a big way.

The film's trailer, which began showing in theaters and online in early 2005, is simply enchanting. If the final film lives up to the public's heightened expectations, we will likely see another giant leap forward for the legitimacy of fantasy films in Hollywood. This time, though, unlike *The Lord of the Rings* with its three films, the Chronicles of Narnia will offer seven films, if Disney decides not to compress two films into one.

Though *The Magician's Nephew* is chronologically the first book in the series, the decision to start this film franchise off with the first published book in the series makes sense. Of the seven books, *The Lion, the Witch and the Wardrobe* is the most popular, the most enduring, and the one most likely to appeal to the greatest possible audience. Disney has already committed to two more films, so they are assuredly thinking long-term.

I wish upon a star that Disney will have a huge success with the film franchise because it will inevitably bring new fans to the fold, sending book sales soaring, reaching new heights. That is a good thing. At a time when electronic gadgets of every kind demand attention and draw potential readers away from the magic of the printed word, film franchises like *The Lord of the Rings* and the Chronicles of Narnia command attention and turn passive viewers into active readers.

As with *The Lord of the Rings*, Lewis's Chronicles have much to offer. And, as with *The Lord of the Rings*, it's best to keep in mind that the film is an adaptation, while the primary works are the novels themselves. Those who wish to truly explore Middle-earth and Narnia are best advised to read the books and discover what readers have known for more than a half century: these well-told tales hold our attention and instill in us a sense of wonder. That is the true magic of Narnia.

If you have come to these books for the first time, you are in for a treat. Just open the wardrobe, draw back the coats, and push in further. You will soon feel the snow underfoot and a bracing winter blast. Just walk toward the lamppost, but remember your way back, and don't forget: if you get lost, ask for Mr. Tumnus. He's a faun, and if you find him, you have indeed found your way to Lewis's enchanting world of Narnia.

C. S. Lewis's Views on Writing for Children

IT's A CURIOUS THING, but it speaks volumes: In England, the Harry Potter novels are issued in two editions—one with a dust jacket specifically drawn to appeal to children, and the other with a dust jacket specifically drawn to appeal to adults who somehow feel it demeaning to be seen in public reading a children's book. (Stateside, Scholastic Books issues a single edition.)

I don't think Lewis would have much sympathy for those adults who feel the need to conceal what they are reading in such a transparent manner.

The question of whether or not the Harry Potter novels are in fact children's books is beyond the scope of my discussion. The fact remains that among the general public and, unfortunately, some writers as well, writing for children means dumbing down the books, deliberately using simple words—in short, patronizing young readers—and going to pains to give the kiddies "what they want."

Lewis had a few run-ins with aspiring writers who shared those antiquated philosophies. (I'm sure those writers' careers never got off the ground.) Lewis himself never had the benefit

49

of having his own children. Because of World War II, however, The Kilns became a refuge for London evacuees—all children. Also, late in life, he became a stepfather to two boys, the sons of Helen Joy Davidman.

The lion's share of Lewis's correspondence came from children, who touched a responsive chord in Lewis; he took their letters seriously and answered them in kind. In fact, a collection of his letters to them was posthumously published as *C. S. Lewis Letters to Children*, which sheds considerable light on many facets of Narnia.

Lewis asserted—quite correctly—that when it comes to children's stories, "the good ones last." Citing his enjoyment late in life of Kenneth Grahame's *The Wind in the Willows*, Lewis made it clear that he didn't make an artificial distinction as a reader between what is commonly known as a children's book and its more grown-up counterparts. As Lewis explained in his famous essay on the subject, "On Three Ways of Writing for Children," "The child as reader is neither to be patronised nor idolised: we talk to him as man to man. The worst attitude of all would be the professional attitude which regards children in the lump as a sort of raw material which we have to handle."

Give the children their due, Lewis states, for that is what they deserve and that's what the work deserves as well.

Unfortunately, not all adults see eye-to-eye with Lewis. To them, children's books should not offend, they should be light in tone, and they should be easy reading. *USA Today* founder, Al Neuharth, writing about the sixth Harry Potter novel, said, "This book is not really for kids. Too much grown-up sex, sin and death replace the youthful charm and intrigue of the earlier Potters." Chiming in agreement, *USA Today* book reviewer Deirdre Donahue wrote, "There is really only one flaw in the sixth installment of J. K. Rowling's series, *Harry Potter and the Half-Blood Prince*: It is not a kids' book." Meaning, as she explained, "the dramatic eternals: betrayal, revenge, death, love, hate, loyalty and sacrifice. OK, this reader thinks these elements are a bit grim for young readers but, hey, I can't wait for Book 7."

Lewis, who wrote of these very things in the Chronicles of Narnia, would likely get into a rousing debate with Neuharth and Donahue because he felt that these are *precisely* the matters that good fiction must address, that this is the world we live in—children and adults alike—and therefore these issues are not only the stuff of fiction but the stuff of life.

Lewis's notions of how to write for children—as opposed to others who feel it necessary to write down to children—go a long way toward explaining why the Chronicles of Narnia has found new readers with each passing generation since 1950, when the first book in the series was published.

Mark Twain once observed that a literary classic was "a book which people praise and don't read."

In the case of Lewis and the Chronicles of Narnia, these are books that people not only praise but have also read, with millions of copies sold to date, and not all of them to children.

COIN DESIGN FOR BARNES & NOBLE

ON THE READING ORDER OF THE CHRONICLES OF NARNIA

The White Rabbit put on his spectacles. "Where shall I begin, please your Majesty?" he asked.

"Begin at the beginning," the King said gravely, "and go on till you come to the end: then stop."

❖ *Alice in Wonderland* by Lewis Carroll

IT'S A SIMPLE ENOUGH QUESTION that has befuddled Narnia fans for years. Simply put: In what order should the books be read?

The Lewis community is divided into two camps: those who believe the books should be read in the order of original publication, and those who believe the books should be read in chronological order.

That the books should be read in the order they were originally published is a view held by some of the most well-known names in the field of Lewis criticism. This means that *The Lion, the Witch and the Wardrobe* should be the first book to be read. Besides, they say, Disney is releasing its film version as the first in a projected series of film adaptations of the Chronicles of Narnia, so isn't that all the more reason to read them in such fashion?

At first glance, that seems a sensible enough approach, except that it recalls the convoluted story of the *Star Wars* films, in which director George Lucas released episodes four through six, followed by episodes one through three. Now that all six installments are available on DVD, most people will view them chronologically because the story makes more sense. At the heart of *Star Wars* is the story of Anakin Skywalker (aka Darth Vader) and his fall from grace. The story begins with Anakin Skywalker's humble beginnings as a slave on a remote planet and ends in his eventual destruction, along with that of the dark empire he served.

Other Lewis fans and scholars maintain that the books should be read in chronological order, beginning with *The Magician's Nephew*, in which Digory Kirke and Polly Plummer use magic rings to travel to the Wood Between the Worlds and beyond.

In fact, chapter 15 of *The Magician's Nephew* is titled, "The End of This Story and the Beginning of All the Others," which makes it clear that this is where the Narnia story cycle properly begins.

The chronological approach is favored by Lewis's American publisher, who asserts that "Although *The Magician's Nephew* was written several years after Lewis first began the Chronicles of Narnia, he wanted it to be read as the first book in the series. HarperCollins is happy to present these books in the order in which Professor Lewis preferred."

As for Professor Lewis, what was *his* opinion? In a letter to a boy named Lawrence, who in 1957 asked that very question—in which order should the books be read?—Lewis responded:

> I think I agree with your order (i.e., chronological) for reading the books more than with your mother's. The series was not planned beforehand as she thinks. When I wrote *The Lion* I did not know I was going to write any more. Then I wrote *P. Caspian* as a sequel and still didn't think there would be any more, and when I had done *The Voyage* I felt quite sure it would be the last. But I found as I was wrong. So perhaps it does not matter very much in which order anyone reads them. I'm not even sure that all the others were written in the same order in which they were published.

Well, there you have it. Lewis can be considered the final authority on this issue; and if he says the reading order is not critical, then it isn't. Therefore, why not read them from start to finish in chronological fashion?

In the end, what's really important is simply reading the books. Let the critics debate this until the end of Narnia; the rest of us won't worry about it—we'll be too busy reading.

Into and Out of the Wardrobe
(WITH APOLOGIES TO C. S. LEWIS)

ONCE UPON A TIME a ten year-old girl named Hannah found herself, much against her wishes, in Wheaton, Illinois, where her mother had a job interview at Wheaton College as a librarian.

Since Hannah's father was busy with his "investments" (whatever *that* meant, thought Hannah), and he was in his own world, especially when parked in front of his computer, where he monitored the rise and fall in the stock market, Hannah's mother sensibly brought her along and hoped she could stay out of trouble. Hannah would have preferred to stay home, curled up in bed with overstuffed pillows and a book, with her cats.

Not that Hannah was a bad seed—indeed, Hannah was the very model of good behavior—but, like her two cats Fili and Kili who got into everything, especially balls of yarn and sheets of newspaper, Hannah was filled to the brim with curiosity. "I just have to know," she'd say, as if that would explain everything to her mother, who would shake her head and wonder where she got such fanciful ideas—probably from her husband, who had a touch of fancy about him.

Even in the cavernous and silent rooms of the library, where the only sounds that could be heard were the slow turning of pages and the gentle hiss of the central air conditioning, Hannah found herself wondering just what was so interesting in the books that the old men—professors, she had been told—were reading.

So, quite naturally, Hannah would tug on her mother's hand to steer her toward the nearest table, occupied by professorial gentlemen who, in truth, would have been charmed by Hannah's interest. One, in particular, smiled broadly as he saw the child tugging at her mother.

Hannah's mother put an end to any such thoughts. "There's no disturbing the professors!" she said, as she pulled the small child along, like a pull toy.

In a large library room at the Marion E. Wade Center, which was where Hannah's mother would be working if she got the job, a large wardrobe stood, commanding her attention. At seven feet high, it towered above the little blond girl, and at four feet across, it was big enough for her to enter, if she wished.

Its size alone would warrant attention, but the doors with their curious carvings also interested her, and as she reached forward to touch the wardrobe, she heard her mother's alarmed voice cry out, "Hannah, don't touch that!"

Hannah's mother turned to the head librarian—a tall man named Mr. Kirke, who smiled knowingly at the small child—and said, "I'm so sorry! Hannah's just the most curious little girl." Yadda, yadda, yadda, Hannah's mother continued, as she became more distracted and Hannah walked up to the rather curious wardrobe and read the small, neatly printed sign prominently posted on a nearby riser: "Enter at your own risk. The Wade Center assumes no responsibility for persons who disappear or who are lost in this wardrobe."

Well, that means you can go in, thought Hannah, but why, she thought, would the sign use the words disappear and lost?

It was an altogether curious matter, but soon things would become curiouser and curiouser. With her mother in another world—she was *always* in another world—Hannah opened the large wardrobe doors and saw the usual assortment of coats, but behind them, she saw a light that seemed to come from behind the wardrobe, and so, quite naturally, she had to find out what was there. *Had* to.

She stepped up and inside the wardrobe, as she heard her

mother screaming, "Hannah, *don't* go in there, don't!" But Hannah couldn't hear her mother's voice because it sounded fainter and fainter, and she pushed on and felt something crunching beneath her feet, until she suddenly stepped down and out of the wardrobe, out its back end.

"Where am I?" she said aloud, but she had no idea where she was; moreover, she wasn't quite sure how to get back to her mother—a concern, but not the immediate one.

She ventured farther and saw a lamppost, which she passed as she headed to a crossroad marked with large signs pointing in every direction to places she'd never heard of: Archenland, Ettinsmoor, Western Wild, and a dozen others.

Curiously, the more she looked at the sign, the more signposts appeared with even more names: Beruna, Cair Paravel, the Lone Isles, and more.

Then a nimble-footed faun ran up to her and pressed into her hands a large map that magically unfolded itself, labeled with all sorts of unrecognizable places.

Suddenly, from around the corner, came talking bears, donkeys, apes, mice, cats, flying horses, and eagles—a cacophony of voices, each creature proudly shouting its name. Then came Calormen, Narnians, giants, dwarves, kings, queens, and all sorts of mythological Greek and Roman creatures. Last came one-legged things jumping up and down, thumping loudly.

A magician approached Hannah and knelt down, holding the fattest book she had ever seen. It was bound in leather and had a large metal clasp. It was four inches thick.

"If you want to know about Narnia, this is the book you'll want to read," the magician said. Hannah laid the book on the ground and opened it up. There were no pictures and the print was very small; even worse, the writing was scholarly, and certainly not intended for young readers.

"Thank you," she said, "but it's really more than I want to read. Do you have anything shorter?"

The magician laughed. "Maybe you're too young to read this book. But I think I may have something that would be just the thing for you. Open your hands, palms up."

Hannah did so, wondering what he might conjure up. The magician waved a wand and a small paperback book rested lightly on her hands. The book's title read, *The Lion, the Witch and the Wardrobe*.

"This is a good place to start," the magician said. "You really can't go wrong if you begin here."

Hannah smiled. "Are there any more?" she asked.

"There are six more books," the magician replied, "and when you finish this one, it'll magically turn into the next one. That way, it won't seem so intimidating."

Hannah nodded.

In the distance, Hannah heard a voice, one that she immediately recognized. It was the voice of her mother, calling to her. Soon she felt herself being shaken, and the voice of her mother became louder.

She felt herself pulled out of her dream, where she had been to a strange but wonderful place called Narnia.

"Hannah, if you don't get up now, you'll miss the school bus!" her mother said.

That night, as Hannah got ready to go to bed, she found a small book under her pillow. Its title: *The Lion, the Witch and the Wardrobe*. Fili jumped up on the headboard and Kili jumped on the bed and they made themselves comfortable, since Hannah liked to read to them late at night. She held the book in her hands, and the pages turned themselves—maybe she hadn't dreamt of Narnia after all—and she fell asleep, dreaming of a helpful faun named Mr. Tumnus and the kind-hearted Mr. and Mrs. Beaver, and most of all, a magnificent lion named Aslan whose deep roar was so loud that she woke up . . . to the sound of a motorcycle revving up.

A Narnian Primer for the Newcomer

KIRK

THE NEWCOMER TO NAR-
NIA may be intimidated, and
understandably so. To truly
understand and appreciate
Narnia in all its wonder, you
must read the books. They are
available in a one-volume edition, collecting all seven novels
that comprise the Chronicles
of Narnia, which totals 767
pages of small type (movie
tie-in edition, HarperCollins).
Furthermore, the single best reference on Narnia, by Paul F. Ford,
is 530 pages of small type, with hundreds of detailed, cross-in-
dexed entries, arranged alphabetically from *Adam* to *Zardeenah*.

It also helps to read a book or two (or three) about Lewis and
Narnia. Most such works are scholarly in tone and filled with
lots of pages of small type. . . .

No wonder some fans just prefer to wait for the movie, which
is finally coming out in December 2005. But the movie really
isn't the book, so the true Narnian at heart should be prepared to
put in the hours to read the principal and secondary texts.

Fortunately, it's not like homework—this assignment is one
you will enjoy.

Here, then, is what you *really* need to know before you start
reading Lewis's Narnian Chronicles.

Creation of Narnia

Aslan created Narnia from an unformed world, its creation witnessed by four humans (and one horse) from London, England, and an evil person from another planet.

The four people, whom we meet in *The Magician's Nephew*, are: Andrew Ketterly (a magician whose lust for unearned knowledge proves to have disastrous consequences); his nephew Digory Kirke (a young boy who is tricked by his uncle to go on a search-and-rescue mission); a new friend of Digory's, Polly Plummer (whom Digory is sent to rescue); and Frank, who drives a cab pulled by his horse, Strawberry. With them is a wicked witch named Jadis, the last empress of Charn, who goes with Digory Kirke and Polly Plummer to London and wreaks havoc, then goes with them, as does Frank and his horse, to an unformed world that will become Narnia.

Narnia—the land and all its creatures—was created in magnificent fashion by Aslan. The pure world was tainted from the beginning, however, by the presence of Jadis, who subsequently fled from Aslan to head north. There she became the White Witch, putting a century-long winter enchantment on Narnia until Aslan comes to Narnia's rescue.

Aslan gave Strawberry the gift of speech and the gift of flight. With those gifts, the dumb horse received a new name (Fledge), and, like Pegasus, wings so that he could soar. Aslan also gave some of the other animals near-human intelligence and the gift of speech.

Geography

Narnia refers to the world of Narnia itself, which is flat, and to the country of Narnia, which has two other major countries nearby: Archenland to its south and, further south, Calormen.

The capital of Narnia is Cair Paravel, located on its eastern edge, flanking the Eastern Ocean, which has numerous islands and archipelagoes, including Galma to the east and Terebinthia to the southeast. Even farther east lie the Seven Isles, the Lone Islands, and the unchartable region beyond.

Narnia's royalty includes kings, queens, emperors, lords, dukes, and barons.

North of Narnia: the land of the giants, the Wild Waste Lands of the North, and Ettinsmoor. As recounted in *The Silver Chair*, the giants are scattered throughout both areas, though a community of them can be found in Harfang, which was visited by Jill Pole, Eustace Scrubb, and a lugubrious but helpful Narnian creature called Puddleglum.

West of Narnia is Lantern Waste and, farther west, the Western Wild. Little is known about the Western Wild except that it lives up to its name. Lewis tells us little about this forsaken region.

There exists one other region in Narnia: Underland. Its name is suggestive of its location, for it is literally located under land—specifically, under Narnia. It is a region ruled by the serpentine Queen of Underland, who wields an iron fist, as recounted in *The Silver Chair*.

Beneath Underland is Bism, a land occupied by gnomes, whom Polly and Digory meet.

Narnia's history is largely peaceful, with occasional upheavals: a long period of perpetual winter, the result of an evil enchantment from the White Witch, and invasions from the country of Calormen.

Archenland is principally mountainous; running east to west, the Winding Arrow river lies south of Archenland. Its people have historically been at peace with the country of Narnia.

Farther south, across the Great Desert, is Calormen, whose people are swarthy. They worship an ugly, four-armed birdlike god named Tash, who makes his frightening appearance in *The Last Battle*.

Time

Narnia exists from Narnia Year 1 (chronicled in *The Magician's Nephew*) to Narnia Year 2555 (chronicled in *The Last Battle*). Time is relative in Narnia: that is to say, only 49 years pass on Earth, but during that same time, 2,555 years pass in Narnia. So, as children from our world go to Narnia, they are surprised—until they understand how quickly time passes there—to find that people they knew as children, who were their age, are now full-grown adults, many of them seniors.

This is why, when Lucy returned from Narnia after having tea with Mr. Tumnus, in *The Lion, the Witch and the Wardrobe,* she felt it had been the better part of an afternoon, but her siblings at Professor Kirke's house simply never noticed her absence, for to them only minutes passed.

Though time does pass in Narnia, it doesn't in the Wood Between the Worlds (a place visited by Polly Plummer and Digory Kirke in *The Magician's Nephew*) or, of course, in Aslan's Country.

The Wood Between the Worlds is actually a passageway to other, uncounted worlds. With the exception of Charn (described in *The Magician's Nephew*), we know nothing about these other worlds.

Time Frame

In speech, dress, customs, and government, Narnia resembles medieval England, with its chivalry, emphasis on honor, and duty to the king.

Cosmology

The stars in the sky tell all, if only they could speak. But in Narnia, actually, they do: The stars are not remote celestial bodies but, in fact, living beings that occasionally fall to Narnia.

In *The Last Battle*, this becomes a key component to understanding the events that unfold. The stars were created by Aslan and answer to him.

Inhabitants

Among the world of humans in Narnia, it's the Calormenes who are the troublemakers. In *The Horse and His Boy* and, more significantly, *The Last Battle*, the Calormenes show their true colors: they seek to dominate Narnia at all costs.

The Telmarines are not an indigenous race—their ancestors were pirates who went through a cave to emerge in Narnia. Intermingling with natives in the western mountains, the Telmarines are the New Narnians, who invade and conquer Narnia in Narnian Year 1998. Not unexpectedly, the New Narnians hate the Old Narnians—the original inhabitants, including both talking and nontalking beasts and mythological creatures of every description.

Dwarves also play a significant role in Narnia. Aslan calls them Sons of Earth because of their affinity for mining and love of subterranean realms. The red-haired dwarves are generally good and the black-haired dwarves are generally bad. (The favorite saying among the black-haired dwarves is "The dwarves are for the dwarves.") In other words, they are self-centered.

Animals

There are talking animals and "dumb" animals. The talking animals are the ones on whom Aslan bestowed the gift of speech in Narnia Year 1, recounted in *The Magician's Nephew*.

In *The Last Battle*, the talking animals, who prefer freedom to everything else, are hoodwinked by one of their own, a devious ape named Shift, who puts a lion's skin on another talking animal, a gentle donkey named Puzzle, and convinces the other talking beasts that Aslan has returned: a blasphemous lie that does not go unnoticed.

The "dumb" animals, despite their nontalking status, are honored and treated with respect, though they can be hunted for food.

Narnia is populated by a representative sampling of the animal kingdom: mice, beavers, hedgehogs, rabbits, moles, horses and donkeys, birds, dogs, cats, and bears.

Narnia is also home to legendary creatures, many of them from Greco-Roman or northern mythology. Their physical appearance is usually suggestive of their intent: the ugly creatures are bad, and the more attractive creatures are good.

Good creatures: centaurs, dryads, fauns, gnomes, hamadryads, maenads, naiads, winged horses, phoenix, satyrs, star people, and unicorns.

Bad creatures: boggles, cruels, efreets, dragons, ghouls, hags, horrors, incubi, minotaurs, ogres, orknies, people of the toadstools, spectres, sprites, werewolves, witches, wooses, and wraiths.

There are also creatures called Marsh-wiggles (Puddleglum is the only one we know; his story is recounted in *The Silver Chair*) and the Monopods (also known as Duffers), who are very simple creatures, lacking maturity and wisdom.

Father Christmas (in *The Lion, the Witch and the Wardrobe*) and Father Time (in *The Silver Chair* and *The Last Battle*) are in a category unto themselves, as each plays significant, unique roles in the events that shape Narnia.

In terms of gods, there is the god of the Calormenes, the false god Tash, who is a large, manlike creature with four arms and a birdlike beak (in *The Last Battle*).

There is also Aslan, the Lion King, whose father is called the Emperor-Beyond-the-Sea, meaning the Eastern Sea. Aslan is the personification of Jesus—a connection Lewis felt was more easily accepted, and grasped, by children as opposed to adults, as he pointed out in a 1963 letter to a girl named Ruth, when he wrote: "If you continue to love Jesus, nothing much can go wrong with you, and I hope you may always do so. I'm so thankful you realized [the] 'hidden story' in the Narnian books. It is odd, children nearly always do, grown-ups hardly ever."

The Pevensie Children

Transported to Narnia through the wardrobe (as recounted in *The Lion, the Witch and the Wardrobe*), the four Pevensie children—Peter, Susan, Edmund, and Lucy—fulfill the prophecy feared by the White Witch: they assume their thrones in Cair Paravel and rule during Narnia's Golden Age.

Peter, the oldest, is known as High King Peter the Magnificent; his siblings also assume positions of royalty, but he holds the highest rank. Like Aslan, the Pevensie children are a major component of the Narnian Chronicles, but unlike Aslan, they don't appear in all seven of the books.

In addition to the Pevensie children, the others who travel to Narnia include Polly Plummer, Digory Kirke, Eustace Scrubb, and Jill Pole.

They appear in the following books:

1. *The Magician's Nephew:* Polly Plummer and Digory Kirke.

2. *The Lion, the Witch and the Wardrobe:* All four Pevensie children.

3. *The Horse and His Boy:* Susan Pevensie, Edmund Pevensie.

4. *Prince Caspian:* All four Pevensie children.

5. *The Voyage of the* Dawn Treader: Edmund Pevensie, Lucy Pevensie, Eustace Scrubb.

6. *The Silver Chair:* Eustace Scrubb and Jill Pole.

7. *The Last Battle:* Eustace Scrubb, Jill Pole, Polly Plummer, Digory Kirke, and all the Pevensie children except Susan; collectively, they are known as the Friends of Narnia.

The End of Narnia

All good things must come to an end, and in *The Last Battle*, we learn the fate of Narnia, which has existed for 2,555 Narnian years. Even when Aslan created Narnia, he had planned for its end—its transformation—and in one of the most moving chapters of *The Last Battle*, we watch cosmic events unfold that, in their terrible beauty, cannot be understated, as night falls for the last time in Narnia, which becomes (literally and figuratively) the Shadowlands.

THE MAGICIAN'S NEPHEW
(1955)

It is a very important story because it shows how all the comings and goings between our own world and the land of Narnia first began.

❖Chapter 1: "The Wrong Door" in *The Magician's Nephew*

Background

Lewis's original title: *Polly and Digory.*

Autobiographical Element

When Lewis was only nine years old, his mother died of cancer. In this book, we see Lewis work through his pain—the healing art of fiction—by writing about a similar dilemma faced by Digory Kirke, whose mother is dying as the doctors watch helplessly. With the help of Aslan, however, Digory's mother recovers to full strength—a miracle, say her doctors. But Digory knows better: It is the power of Aslan and everything he represents that restores health to his mother.

Reading this book first, as opposed to reading the first published book in the series (*The Lion, the Witch and the Wardrobe*), orients the reader by establishing a firm groundwork for what is to follow.

The book begins with an impromptu, albeit uneasy, friendship between Polly Plummer and Digory Kirke, two children who live in London. Naturally curious, the children, who live in row houses with attic crawl spaces that allow them to go from house to house, go exploring and find themselves in what they think is an open room. In fact, it's the private room of Digory Kirke's eccentric uncle, Andrew Ketterly, who fancies himself a magician of sorts.

Ketterly qualifies as a magician, but just barely; he recognizes the magical qualities of the dust contained in a box from Atlantis, which belonged to his godmother. From the dust he fashions several pairs of rings in two colors: yellow and green. He mistakenly believes the yellow ring is for an outbound journey to what he calls the Other Place, and the green ring is for an inbound journey back home.

Ketterly, who has no mastery of magic, is clearly a dabbler, and proves the old adage that a little knowledge is a dangerous thing. His scant knowledge isn't enough to inform him of the truth: the yellow ring will transport the bearer to a place called the Wood Between the Worlds, for that is where the yellow dust that comprises the ring wishes to go, back to its original home; and the green ring will transport the reader into another world, but not necessarily Ketterly's London, England.

The presumptuous, and cowardly, Ketterly tricks Polly into touching a yellow ring, and she goes off to a place unknown. A horrified Digory Kirke shouts out to warn her, but it is too late.

Now, the only possibility of saving her is if he, too, touches a yellow ring to be transported to what Ketterly mistakenly calls the Other Place. The ring, of course, transports the bearer to the Wood Between the Worlds, which is where Digory finds Polly. Both are understandably disoriented and have only the faintest recollections of who the other is. But the discovery of the yellow rings on their fingers awakens their memories: they know who they are and how they got there. The question is, how can they get back?

The pools around them are portals to other worlds, and after transporting themselves back to their own place and time, they linger long enough to recognize how to get home, and then switch to yellow rings to take them back to the Wood Between the Worlds, a way station. They mark that pool with a strip of turf and then go exploring.

Hand in hand, they leap into another pool and find themselves in Charn, a dead world. When Digory calls it a "queer place," he is correct. It is like no place he's ever seen. It is preternaturally quiet, and as they explore this increasingly forbidding, and foreboding, world, they see hundreds of seated people, all frozen in time.

Magic, they realize, is at play here; and as they go down the row of richly dressed people, they see that their facial expressions are uniformly proud but cruel, and increasingly reflect despair.

In the last occupied seat is a tall, beautiful woman of regal bearing. She is to Digory the most beautiful woman he has ever seen, though Polly doesn't share his opinion.

Questions abound: Why is this world so dead? Why are these rulers immobilized? Who are these people? The answers become apparent when temptation proves too much for Digory. Reading a poem that challenges him to find out or go mad wondering—to strike the bell or not, that is the dilemma—Digory foolishly holds Polly's wrist, preventing her from reaching for her yellow ring, and when he strikes the bell with the hammer, he unwittingly sets into motion a chain of events that will reverberate through the long, colorful history of Narnia.

Biting the forbidden fruit, so to speak, Digory's curiosity literally brings down the house. The sound of hammer against bell grows loud, and louder still. Finally, when the sound stops, the children are surprised to find out that the ringing of the bell has broken the spell binding Jadis, an Empress, and the only survivor of her world.

Imperious and cruel, condescending and deprecating, Jadis shows her true colors. She destroyed her world and all living things in it except herself by speaking the Deplorable Word. Jadis is victorious, but at what cost? She reigns over a dead world that cannot be resurrected. She now wants to take over another world, one occupied by living persons and creatures—the world of Digory Kirke and Polly Plummer.

Despite their attempts to shake Jadis off, she holds on to Polly's hair and is transported to the Wood Between the Worlds. As Polly and Digory soon realize, it's not necessary to have a ring for transport; merely touching a person with a ring also allows transport. She follows them to their own world by grabbing Digory's ear.

Back in London, Uncle Andrew—amazed at the children's return, and even more amazed at the tall, regal witch—shows his true colors by obsequiously placing himself at her disposal, which she feels is simply her due.

After running amok in London, Jadis, ripping a crossbar off a lamppost, uses it to attack a policeman. The crowd witnessing this gathers to attack her, and Digory and Polly transport the lot of them—themselves, Jadis, Digory's Uncle Andrew, a cabby and his horse Strawberry—to the Wood Between the Worlds and finally to an "empty world. This is Nothing," states Jadis, and she is correct.

But something is at work on Nothing. It is here that Aslan sings his creation song and Narnia gloriously takes form. Not only does the geography of Narnia come into being, but so do its creatures and everything else.

Through Aslan, Digory redeems himself. After bringing evil in the form of Jadis to Narnia, Digory is sent by Aslan on a mission to find a magic apple in the mountains of the Western Wild. Flying on Fledge (the former Strawberry, the hansom-cab horse who can now speak and fly, gifts from Aslan), Digory and Polly retrieve the magic apple; from it, a tree grows that protects Narnia from Jadis. Everything that is good about the tree is anathema to Jadis. She flees to the north, where she will gather her strength, marshal her resources, and bide her time, "growing stronger in dark magic" (writes Lewis), until she fulfills her destiny—one that Aslan has foreseen. She will become known as the White Witch; cold-hearted and cruel, she will place all of Narnia under a chilly enchantment for a century.

The tree is not the only thing that grows in the fertile soil of Narnia. The iron crossbar from the lamppost, buried in the ground, yields a new lamppost in the area of Narnia now dubbed Lantern Waste. Located northeast of the location of the Wardrobe, the lamppost is the fixture that will orient the Pevensie children to the Wardrobe and back to their own world.

Digory returns home to London with an apple from the Tree and, feeding it to his dying mother, saves her life. He buries the apple core in their backyard, and from it springs a tree with beautiful apples. But when the tree is blown down, its precious, and magical, wood is used by him years later to construct a wardrobe. It will prove to be a magical wardrobe, the gateway from our world to Narnia.

Early in the book, we meet Jadis, who will become the White Witch who casts a spell over Narnia. Late in the book, we meet Aslan, who will be her nemesis. And, at the end of the book, we see the construction of the enchanted wardrobe. All three—the lion, the witch, and the wardrobe—will, of course, figure prominently in the next book.

Key Characters

Polly Plummer has the distinction of being the first human to see the Wood Between the Worlds; she's also one of the first humans to enter Narnia. She is a practical person who knows there's a reason why she shouldn't ring the bell. Also, unlike Digory Kirke, she isn't blinded by Jadis's beauty because she sees only her terrible aspects.

Digory Kirke, like his uncle (Andrew Ketterly), is naturally curious, and to a fault. Just as his uncle blindly seeks knowledge without mastery, Digory seeks answers without temperance. The result of Digory's impetuousness has long-reaching consequences: evil, in the form of Jadis, comes to Narnia, at great cost to those who live there.

On a mission from Aslan, Digory redeems himself by resisting not only the lure of the magical apple, but Queen Jadis's entreaties as well. She promises him great knowledge, eternal life, and high office, all of which he refuses. He chooses mortality, puts his faith in Aslan, and is rewarded. He can return home with his heart's desire: a cure for his dying mother. He has, in Aslan's eyes, redeemed himself.

Jadis is the last survivor of Charn (a word suggestive of charnel, which is short for charnel house, a place associated with death). Defeating the former queen, her sister, by uttering the Deplorable Word, Jadis won a pyrrhic victory.

A monstrous entity, the offspring of a giant and the demon Lilith, Jadis is unadulterated evil. A destroyer, she leaves behind her dying world to find new worlds to conquer, and through an unwitting Digory Kirke is brought to Narnia, introducing evil in an untainted world.

She will become known in the Chronicles of Narnia as the White Witch, held at bay only by the power of the Tree of Protection, though she puts all of Narnia into an eternal winter and draws those of evil natures to her side.

Andrew Ketterly is Digory Kirke's uncle. A dabbler in magic

who fancies himself a genius, he puts himself above all others and harnesses the power of the magical rings without knowing what consequences will result. Arrogant, selfish, and cowardly, he refuses to find out firsthand where the rings may take him. In his place, he deliberately sends Polly Plummer, a young girl. Ketterly tricks her into wearing the ring, which transports her into the Other Place, not knowing what dangers she may face. (Better her than me, he thinks.)

Predictably, Ketterly cowers and simpers in front of Jadis, who soon realizes that he's not the great and powerful magician she thought he must be because of his fashioning the rings that transport her to his world. Similarly, he is cowed by the talking animals—especially by Aslan—none of whom he can understand. He perceives all of them to be beasts, when he in fact is a beastly man.

Aslan is the central figure in this book, and the only character to appear in all the Narnia books. The lion king, Aslan, is wise and omnipotent but appears terrible to those who are evil at heart and incur his considerable wrath. With his creation song, he literally populates Narnia with all manner of living things, recalling Tolkien's *The Silmarillion*.

Clearly allegorical in nature, Aslan, as Lewis explained in a letter to fifth graders in Maryland, is rich in religious symbolism. "Let us suppose that there were a land like Narnia and that the Son of God, as He became a Man in our world, became a Lion there, and then imagine what would happen."

THE LION, THE WITCH AND THE WARDROBE

And that is the very end of the adventure of the wardrobe. But if the Professor was right, it was only the beginning of the adventures of Narnia.

> ❖ the last paragraph of the final chapter ("The Hunting of the White Stag") in *The Lion, the Witch and the Wardrobe*

THE BEST KNOWN OF ALL THE NARNIA NOVELS and the first children's book Lewis wrote, this book is for readers the traditional passageway to Narnia for several reasons. It is the first published book in the series; it is the first appearance of the Pevensie children in Narnia; and in Narnian time, it follows *The Magician's Nephew*, which lays the groundwork for the other books in the series.

As is often the case with writers, the germ of the story took a long time to yield fruit. In 1939, when London evacuated

children to the countryside because of the justifiable fears surrounding Hitler and his bombing campaign against the city, The
Kilns (C. S. Lewis's home, which he shared with his brother and
with Maureen Moore and her mother) played host to the young
evacuees.

The envisioned story: Evacuees from London come out to
the country to stay with a kindly professor.

It was the germ of a story idea that, nearly a decade later,
took final shape as *The Lion, the Witch and the Wardrobe*, the first
of seven novels that would come to be known as the Chronicles
of Narnia, a phrase that was coined not by Lewis but by his former student, then friend, and later biographer, Roger Lancelyn
Green, in 1952. (Lewis himself liked to call them the Narnian
Chronicles.)

After listening with great interest to a fellow professor's stories—J. R. R. Tolkien's tales of Middle-earth—Lewis hoped for
a similar response in return when he read from his work in progress, *The Lion, the Witch and the Wardrobe*. Unfortunately, Lewis
found no ready audience in Tolkien, who found little to like in
the work. Undaunted, Lewis read the work to Roger Lancelyn
Green, then a postgraduate student. Unlike Tolkien, Green was
positively enthusiastic and urged Lewis to continue. Green, who
would later write a study of children's literature titled *Tellers of
Tales*, knew a well-told story when he heard it. He was convinced, unlike Tolkien, that *The Lion, the Witch and the Wardrobe*
was the work of a master storyteller.

Tolkien's Middle-earth was essentially a work of sub-creation,
the construction of a fully realized secondary world, and one in
which a grand design emerged, incorporating the Four Ages of
Middle-earth, as related in *The Silmarillion*, *The Hobbit*, and *The
Lord of the Rings*. In contrast, Lewis had no such grand plan.
Indeed, in approach, Lewis was more a storyteller who wrote the
Narnia novels as they occurred to him.

Even still, the seven novels share a commonality, the presence of Aslan, who is the unifying force of all seven novels. As Colin Duriez quotes Lewis in *A Field Guide to Narnia*, regarding the first Narnia novel, "Aslan came bounding into it. . . . Once He was there He pulled the whole story together, and soon He pulled the six other Narnian stories after him."

In *The Lion, the Witch and the Wardrobe*, we see unmistakable echoes of Lewis's own life: the Pevensie children mirror the evacuees in 1939 who showed up at his home; the kindly professor who takes in those children is mirrored by himself; the enchanted wardrobe is mirrored by the wardrobe constructed by his grandfather, outside of which he sat as a child and told stories to those who sat in it and listened with rapt attention.

In the first chronicle of Narnia, the youngest (and most innocent) of the Pevensie children, Lucy, finds herself opening the wardrobe and walking through it to Narnia, where she meets Mr. Tumnus, a faun, who appears to be a friend but, in fact, is serving the White Witch, who has commanded him to bring to her any human children he encounters, whom she calls the Sons of Adam and the Daughters of Eve.

The White Witch, recalling an ancient prophecy in which the four thrones in Cair Paravel are occupied by the children, thus signaling her demise, seeks to prevent the prophecy from its inevitable fulfillment.

Mr. Tumnus, though, has a change of heart and, rather than sacrificing Lucy to the evil witch, he guides her safely back to the lamppost, where she finds her way home.

Knowing full well that he will be found out, Mr. Tumnus rightly fears that the White Witch will turn him to stone as a permanent reminder of what happens to those who betray her.

When Lucy returns after an extended period in Narnia, she assumes the same passage of time has occurred in the real world, but it has not. Playing a game of hide-and-seek, Lucy's siblings understandably discount her assertion that her prolonged absence was due to a corresponding stay in Narnia; they dismiss her story, but are curious enough to check it out for themselves. Sure enough, the wardrobe appears to be perfectly ordinary and not magical at all.

Of her siblings, it is her brother Edmund who is the most skeptical, until he follows and watches her disappear in the wardrobe. Instead of finding his sister, he finds the self-proclaimed Queen of Narnia, the White Witch, who deliberately feeds him enchanted candy, Turkish delight, which he soon craves at all costs. The price for more: return to Narnia with his brother and two sisters—not one or two, but all three, without exception.

Taken in by the witch's false promises and hungering for more Turkish delight, Edmund readily agrees to do her bidding. It will be, as it was for Digory Kirke in a similar circumstance, a transformation from innocence to experience.

Though Edmund knows the truth, that a world does indeed exist beyond the wardrobe, he deliberately conceals his knowledge of it, and the fact that he is in an alliance with the White Witch, whom Lucy cautions him against, citing Mr. Tumnus's heartfelt fears. Blinded to the truth and anxious to eat all the Turkish delight he's been promised, Edmund doesn't tell his young sister that he in fact has even met the White Witch. He plays the part well, even to the point that when they both return to the real world, he again mocks Lucy for her belief in the existence of Narnia, her tearful protests notwithstanding.

Concerned about Lucy, her brother Peter and sister Susan go see the kindly professor, who uses logic to explain to them that Lucy is not, as they feared, going crazy; she is telling the plain truth.

Peter and Susan discover that truth when they, along with Lucy and Edmund, hide out in the wardrobe to avoid being seen by the housekeeper and her guests. It's a hideout that proves to be a good one, for they suddenly find themselves in Narnia.

What follows is a classic tale of good versus evil, as the

children find allies in the animals of Narnia, including a friendly bird, a robin, and Mr. and Mrs. Beaver, who guide the children to the only power that can save them and Mr. Tumnus as well. The journey takes them to Aslan—all except Edmund, who has deserted them in search of the White Witch, whom he erroneously believes will reward him for news of his siblings in Narnia.

Edmund eventually sees the light, discovering that his treachery exacts an unspeakably high price, but one that will lead to his eventual redemption.

The best-known and most-loved of all the Narnia tales, *The Lion, the Witch and the Wardrobe* was, to Walden Media's and Disney's thinking, the logical choice to kick off what they hope will be an enduring, and lucrative, film franchise that will eclipse *The Lord of the Rings*. With seven Narnia novels to be turned into movies, as opposed to the three movies that comprise *The Lord of the Rings*, Narnia may indeed prove to have staying power, but it's too early to tell.

In this novel, children are forced to evacuate from their home to a stranger's house out in the country, where a stern housekeeper is constantly dictating the rules.

This novel works its magic as an enchanting story in its own right, and as a rite-of-passage story (the children must confront their fears and overcome them in order to learn from their experiences and grow up). It also works as an allegorical tale that touches on the numinous, the cosmic, with the presence of Aslan, a Christ-like figure who is at the heart of this and all the other Narnia novels to come.

Key Characters

Edmund Pevensie: In the beginning of the book, he shows that he has much to learn. Initially dismissive of his sister Lucy's claims that she has been to Narnia, he subsequently follows her into Narnia, only to meet the White Witch, who plies him with false promises and enchanted candy. In time, though, Edmund realizes the truth. Once he sees her as she truly is, he has a permanent change of heart and rejoins his siblings. His destiny is to become King Edmund.

Lucy Pevensie: The youngest of the Pevensie children, she is the first to visit Narnia. It is Lucy who receives from Father Christmas a cordial capable of healing wounds—a gift that proves to be useful when Aslan and his followers do battle with the White Witch and her kind. Small but stout of heart and uncommonly brave, Lucy's destiny is to become Queen Lucy the Valiant.

Peter Pevensie: The oldest of the Pevensie children, Peter kills Maugrim after it attacks his sister Susan. His destiny is not only to become King Peter the Magnificent, but also to be the High King of Narnia.

Susan Pevensie: Gentle and kind with a sweet disposition, Susan proves to be a warrior in her own right, uncommonly skilled with the bow and arrow. In time of need, she has a horn to blow that will call help to her aid—a gift from Father Christmas. She is known as Queen Susan the Gentle.

Mr. Tumnus: Initially in the employment of the White Witch, this kindhearted faun meets Lucy Pevensie on her first trip through the wardrobe and befriends her—or so she thinks. Smitten by Lucy, Mr. Tumnus has a change of heart and tells her the truth, that he was hired to betray her to the White Witch. Together they rush back to the lamppost, and Lucy makes her way home to safety. Mr. Tumnus, though, is not so fortunate. The White Witch turns him to stone.

As to Mr. Tumnus's eventual fate, he is ... well, don't you want to find out for yourself?

Father Christmas: Foreshadowing the arrival of Aslan in Narnia, Santa Claus makes his appearance, bearing useful gifts ("tools, not toys," he explains) for each of the children and for Mrs. Beaver, who left her home and joined her husband, Mr. Beaver, to help the Pevensie children in their search for Aslan. To Peter, he gives a shield and a sword; to Susan, a horn that calls for help when blown, and a bow with a quiver of arrows that will hit their targets; and to Lucy, a little bottle containing a healing cordial, and a dagger as a last resort for self-defense.

Mr. and Mrs. Beaver: Talking animals that befriend the Pevensie children and take them to Aslan. Mr. Beaver is a friend of Mr. Tumnus, the faun.

Maugrim: An evil wolf in the employ of the White Witch, he heads her Secret Police. Peter Pevensie kills Maugrim after the wolf attacks Peter's sister Susan. (Note: He is called Fenris Ulf in the American editions published before 1994.)

Professor Kirke: The child from *The Magician's Nephew*, Digory Kirke, now a college professor, lives in the country and takes in the Pevensie children after they are evacuated from London. Having been to the Wood Between the Worlds and Narnia itself, he affirms to the doubting Peter and Susan that Narnia does indeed exist.

THE HORSE AND HIS BOY

This is the story of an adventure that happened in Narnia and Calormen and the lands between, in the Golden Age when Peter was High King in Narnia and his brother and his two sisters were King and Queens under him.

> ❖ the first paragraph of chapter 1 ("How Shasta Set Out on His Travels") of *The Horse and His Boy*.

Background

ACCORDING TO KATHRYN LINDSKOOG, in *Journey into Narnia*, Lewis and his publisher finally decided on *The Horse and His Boy* after he had proposed to his publisher several alternate titles, including *Shasta and the North*, *The Desert Road to Narnia*, *Cor of Archenland*, *The Horse Stole the Boy*, *Over the Border*, and *The Horse Bree*.

The boy in question is named Shasta, who lives in Calormen with Arsheesh, a poor fisherman. Shasta's daily routine is dull indeed, consisting of drudgery, but occasionally livened with a beating if Arsheesh finds fault, which is a frequent occurence.

Shasta, though, feels a longing he can't satisfy. At times his gaze and thoughts turn northward as he speculates about what life must be like up there. His questions to Arsheesh are hastily deflected. Arsheesh has a very limited worldview; nothing really matters to him, except the number of fish he catches and can sell. And Arsheesh certainly doesn't need probing questions from Shasta that he can't answer, because he's never traveled outside his own small fishing village.

Shasta's life, though, will be changed forever when a tall, dark stranger rides in on his warhorse, demanding, and getting, hospitality from Arsheesh, who can scarcely afford it. When the stranger makes an offer to buy Shasta, Arsheesh sees this as an unexpected, but welcome, opportunity to make a huge profit at Shasta's expense. The rider is a Tarkaan whose name is Anradin.

What ensues verbally between Arsheesh and Anradin is one of the funniest scenes in all of Lewis's fiction, as the two haggle over the amount for which the fisherman will sell Shasta into slavery to the stranger. First, the wheedling Arsheesh asks how could he sell his own son, his own flesh and blood? As Shasta is obviously fair-skinned, with the look of one from the north, and Arsheesh is dark-skinned, it's clear that there's no blood relationship—a fact that Anradin makes abundantly clear. A practical man, Anradin's pointed and piercing words make it clear that he is tolerating the greedy old fool of a fisherman, but just barely. Arsheesh's loquacity is countered by Anradin's blunt truths, and they get down to business to hammer out an agreeable price.

Arsheesh reluctantly tells him the truth, that he found the boy in a boat that washed up on shore, and that the boy was accompanied by a man who had died on the trip. But the boy is of inestimable value to him, so how can he even think of selling him for a pittance?

Shasta, who has overheard all this through a crack in the door, goes outside near the stranger's warhorse to take all of this in. Realizing he is no relation of Arsheesh, he speculates aloud as to what his lineage might be. Stroking the horse's nose, Shasta says he wishes the horse could talk . . . and the horse does.

When the horse, whose name is Breehy-hinny-brinny-hoohy-hah (or Bree, for short), tells Shasta what he's really in for if his master, Anradin, buys him from Arsheesh, Shasta decides that death would be preferable to slavery. It's also clear that Bree is looking to escape and head home to Narnia, if he possibly can.

After determining that both men are asleep, Shasta and Bree make plans to escape, though Bree—a warhorse with no little pride himself—haughtily lectures Shasta on the finer points of riding a horse.

On the road to the north, Shasta and Bree unexpectedly meet other company. They think they are being pursued by lions and by another rider—perhaps a Tarkaan on his warhorse.

They find out they were partially right. Instead of lions, there was one lion; their pursuers turn out to be another horse and rider on the run: a talking mare named Hwin and a girl named Aravis, escaping from a forced marriage.

The four join forces and make their way northward.

A second storyline involves two of the Pevensie children, who, in Narnian time, are now adults. Queen Susan is being courted by Prince Rabadash, who once was her guest at Cair Paravel and pursued her hand in marriage. When she goes to visit him in his capital city, she realizes that he's not what he appears to be—a realization that comes too late.

When Queen Susan and her brother King Edmund are essentially held captive in Rabadash's city of Tashbaan, the capital city of Calormen, they, along with their entourage, make their escape. But they are pursued by Prince Rabadash's formidable army, bent not only on capturing Susan but subjugating the country of Narnia.

A straightforward adventure story that gallops to its end, this novel is filled with excitement, humor, and lessons learned by Shasta (who discovers his real name), by Bree (who learns much about himself and becomes wiser in the process), and by Prince Rabadash, who proves to be a braying fool.

We also learn a lot about Calormen: its culture, its people, and its capital city, Tashbaan.

Main Characters

Shasta: A northern boy who is discovered by Arsheesh, a poor fisherman who found him in a boat.

Arsheesh: A poor fisherman who treats Shasta not as a son

but as a slave, which in fact he is. When the opportunity comes to make a quick buck off Shasta, Arsheesh is eager to sell him at a princely sum to Anradin, a stranger who rides into town. Fond of quoting maxims and proverbs, Arsheesh soon discovers, after Shasta's disappearance, that all he has left are his empty words. Shasta has wised up and headed north, back home.

Bree: A shortened name for Breehy-hinny-brinny-hoohy-hah, Bree is a talking horse that, as a foal, disregarded his mother's warning not to roam the Southern slopes into Archenland, where he was captured and pressed into service. Unbeknown to his master, Anradin, Bree is a talking horse from Narnia—a fact Bree is careful to conceal, because his worth would then be considerably more than that of a normal horse, and he'd be so carefully guarded that eventual escape would be impossible.

Bree, despite his proud talk of his past glories and accomplishments, has much to learn about himself on the journey to the north with Shasta, Hwin, and Aravis.

Hwin: A talking horse ridden by Aravis, Hwin is a mare. Like Bree, she, too, was enslaved when young and pressed into service. Like Bree, who spoke only after Shasta began thinking aloud, Hwin spoke up only when her rider, Aravis, was in despair and about to commit suicide.

Hwin and Aravis make their escape. Both seek freedom: Hwin from slavery and Aravis from a pending forced marriage. They head north, meeting Shasta and Bree on their journey.

Aravis Tarkheena: A determined, young girl from Calormene who was ill-fated to marry the next Grand Vizier, a sixty-year-old man named Ahosta Tarkaan who has the face of an ape and is hunchbacked besides (according to Aravis). She rode Hwin out into the country and prepared to commit suicide by stabbing herself in her heart—an act she didn't commit when, to her great surprise, her mare Hwin said nay.

She and Hwin join forces with Shasta and Bree and head north to escape what are certain to be miserable lives, if others have their way.

Hermit of the Southern March: A magician who befriends Shasta and Aravis, he is 109 years old. A wise man and seer, he knows more than what he lets on; notably, when Aravis suffers superficial wounds, he realizes that it's not luck (to which she attributes her survival) but the hand of a greater power at work, which is indeed the case.

Prince Rabadash: His name is suggestive, rich with meaning. The first half of his name sounds like rabid, which can mean "having a fanatical belief in something"; the second half suggests a stylish or fashionable man. In his case, both are correct. As the oldest son of the eighteen sons of the Tisroc, he is in a prominent position. The crown prince of Calormen, he fanatically pursues Queen Susan, who is initially taken in by his false front (handsome, charming, and agreeable), but soon realizes he's a cruel, arrogant poseur.

In the end, though, Rabadash proves himself less dashing and more rabid. Though he doesn't get what he wants—Queen Susan, Archenland, and Narnia—he does get what he deserves. He is perceived, and rightly so, as nothing more than a braying ass.

PRINCE CASPIAN

Once there were four children whose names were Peter, Susan, Edmund, and Lucy, and it has been told in another book called *The Lion, the Witch and the Wardrobe* how they had a remarkable adventure.

❖ opening paragraph to *Prince Caspian*

Background

ACCORDING TO KATHRYN LINDSKOOG, alternate titles for this book included *Drawn into Narnia*, *A Horn in Narnia*, and *Prince Caspian: The Return to Narnia*.

As the Pevensie children wait at a train station to head off to school, they are inexplicably pulled back into Narnia, not knowing how or why. The luster of their days as rulers of Narnia, in

Cair Paravel during its Golden Age, is long gone. A thousand years have passed in Narnia, and in that time Telmarines from our world have found their way into Narnia, with disastrous consequences for Narnians.

The children are surprised to discover that Cair Paravel is now in ruins. Prince Caspian, who is the rightful heir to the throne, is denied his birthright because of Miraz, the Telmarine king of Narnia. Miraz has pretended affection for his nephew, Prince Caspian, but shows his true colors when his own son and heir is born. Miraz then decides he has no further use for Prince Caspian.

On the run, Prince Caspian is hotly pursued by Miraz, who is bent on hunting him down and killing him, just as he's done to all who stand in his way. Calling himself the Lord Protector, Miraz is simply a despot whose goal is to eliminate any traces of Old Narnia, thus ensuring that his reign, the new order, is unchallenged.

Knowing that Susan's horn can be used to summon help, Prince Caspian blows it, calling the Pevensie children to his will. They are understandably surprised to find themselves back in Narnia.

Aided by Trumpkin, a dwarf who's fond of uttering colorful expressions like "bilge and beanstalks," the Pevensie children and all those true to Old Narnia confront Miraz in an epic battle.

This is the first book in the Prince Caspian trilogy.

Main Characters

Trumpkin: A brave dwarf who is sent by Prince Caspian to aid him and the Old Narnians in a battle against Miraz, the tyrannical king of Narnia. Because he accepts nothing on faith, Trumpkin is initially dismissive of Aslan, whom he has never met. He accepts the children only after Susan proves her skill with bow and arrow, and bests him, to his great surprise.

Prince Caspian: The heart of this book, Prince Caspian is the tenth in a long line of Telmarine kings. An orphan, he is raised by his uncle, the evil Miraz. By all rights, Prince Caspian is the legitimate successor to the throne, but Miraz has other plans.

Dr. Cornelius: A tutor to Prince Caspian, he deliberately hides the fact that he is half human and half dwarf, since he's in truth one of the Old Narnians—the very ones against whom Miraz has waged war. Wise and a truth seeker, Dr. Cornelius appears to be a small human, a perception he encourages because King Miraz would otherwise have him killed.

Miraz: The uncle of Prince Caspian and a king of Narnia, he is one of the Telmarines, a people from our own world who entered Narnia long ago. Miraz is a realist who doesn't believe in magic or in talking animals, and so is at war with the Old Narnians.

Reepicheep: One of the most colorful and endearing creatures in all of Narnia, he is a mouse—small of stature but stout of heart. Diminutive in size, he bristles when anyone suggests anything that he considers an affront to his honor, which he's willing to defend at sword point. Given his size, he's clearly no match for normal-sized people or other creatures who are considerably larger than he is, but that doesn't stop him from throwing himself into any fray. To die in battle would strike him as an honorable death, as he fears not death but dishonor.

In a final battle between the Old and New Narnians, Reepicheep suffers a loss, and thereby hangs a tale . . . er, tail.

THE VOYAGE
OF THE
DAWN TREADER

There was a boy called Eustace Clarence Scrubb, and he almost deserved it.

❖ opening sentence to *The Voyage of the* Dawn Treader

A SEQUEL to *Prince Caspian*, this book recalls Homer's *Odyssey* and Jonathan Swift's *Gulliver's Travels*, with its diary entries and visits to unknown islands. A quest novel, this one recounts the voyage of the *Dawn Treader*, boldly going where no man (or mouse) has gone before, seeking new worlds and new civilizations. . . .

The story begins in a novel way: Lucy and Edmund are in the bedroom of their cousin, Eustace Clarence Scrubb. On the wall in the bedroom is a picture of a sailing ship that takes on an air of reality the more they look at it. As Lucy remarks, "I like it because the ship looks as if it were really moving. And the water looks as if it were really wet. And the waves look as if they were really going up and down."

But when the children are sprayed with seawater, Eustace rushes forward, meaning to tear the picture off the wall and destroy it. Edmund and Lucy follow, knowing magic is at play, and all three children find themselves in the water, struggling for survival, until they are fortuitously plucked out by the crew of the *Dawn Treader*, captained by Drinian.

On board, Prince Caspian is accompanied by the bravest mouse in all of Narnia, the noble, though diminutive, Reepicheep, who has come along on this journey for a private purpose. After his coronation, Prince Caspian vowed to find (if alive) or avenge (if dead) his father's friends, the seven lords who were victimized by the deposed king of Narnia, Miraz: Lord Revilian, Lord Bern, Lord Argoz, Lord Mavramorn, Lord Octesian, Lord Restimar, and Lord Rhoop.

The problem, though, is that carrying out this vow means journeying by sea beyond the boundaries of known Narnia to its outer limits, with no foreknowledge of what may confront, or befall, them.

Reepicheep, the most valiant mouse in all of Narnia, would gladly have gone on this voyage just to assist Prince Caspian, if that was his desire, but the stouthearted mouse is on his own quest. When he was in his cradle, a Dryad (a tree spirit) came to him and recited an enchanting poem telling him that he would find everything he looked for in life in "the utter east." Reepicheep knows his destiny is bound in the four lines of verse uttered by the Dryad, and so is determined to see this voyage to its end.

Though Lucy and Edmund are happy to be back in Narnia, the same cannot be said for their cousin, Eustace Scrubb, who is contentious, self-centered, and, after several days without a bath, in dire need of a good scrubbing. And when the voyage turns perilous and he begins complaining nonstop, it's soon apparent that he's in need of a good drubbing as well.

The *Dawn Treader* heads east, and its stout crew faces the unknown with brave hearts. The voyage is one of personal discovery as much as it is a physical journey. Eustace Scrubb learns a lot about himself; Lucy and Edmund learn a sad truth about themselves and Aslan; Reepicheep's destiny is fulfilled; Prince Caspian's world changes forever; and we see Aslan and learn more about his eternal world.

The Voyage of the Dawn Treader is the second of three books that form the Prince Caspian trilogy.

Main Characters

Eustace Clarence Scrubb: He's the cousin of the Pevensie children, and is a mirror image of them: Where they are kind, courageous, and easy to get along with, he is a bully, a coward, and impossible to get along with; in short, he resembles Dudley Dursley from J. K. Rowling's Harry Potter novels. Quite by accident, he is drawn into Narnia, along with Lucy and Edmund Pevensie. Once there, Eustace (admittedly a rather unfortunate name for a boy) Scrubb suffers trials and tribulations. A beast of a little boy, he undergoes a transformation, both physical and spiritual, and subsequently repents.

The Lord Drinian: The captain of the *Dawn Treader*, he is loyal to Prince Caspian and literally follows him to the end of the world, beyond which Aslan's country can be found.

Gumpas: The governor of the Lone Islands, which is under Narnian rule, he goes by the title of "His Sufficiency" and encourages his island's principal business, slave trading. A career bureaucrat, he refuses to see anyone unless they have an appointment, which can only be scheduled on the second Saturday of each month between 9:00 and 10:00 P.M. In other words, for one hour, at a most inconvenient time, and only once a month! It's his way of discouraging appointments altogether.

Hardly living up to his name (*Gumpas* sounds like *gumption*, which means *being resourceful* or *having initiative*), Governor Gumpas has the unmitigated gall to put off Prince Caspian, King of Narnia, who demands the annual tribute that has gone unpaid for some years—150, to be exact. To that, Gumpas responds, "That would be a question to raise at the Council next month. If anyone moves that a commission of enquiry be set up to report on the financial history of the islands at the first meeting next year, why then . . ." Gumpas is simply oblivious to the situation he finds himself in.

Prince Caspian cuts him off and demands the tribute immediately, out of the governor's own pocket.

Gumpas, like others of his kind, gets his just desserts.

Sea Serpent: After leaving the aptly named Dragon Island, the crew of the Dawn Treader encounter, and barely survive, an encounter with a sea serpent that encircles and attempts to crush their ship.

The Magician: A benevolent wizard who lives on an island principally inhabited by curious creatures. The Magician's real name is Coriakin, and he's a star from the night sky sent to look after the curious island creatures.

The Great Eastern Ocean: The great ocean to the east of Narnia, this is where the *Dawn Treader* boldly goes, seeking out the seven lords, friends of Prince Caspian's father who unaccountably disappeared because of Miraz's machinations.

Ramandu: A star at rest, as he describes himself, he explains to the crew of the *Dawn Treader* what is in store for them as they venture eastward. Ramandu has taken the form of an old man (mirroring his age as a star) and is growing younger with each fire-berry brought to him by a bird; eventually, he will be a young child and, as a star, will rise again, born anew. He lives on an island on Narnia's eastern rim, with his daughter.

The Last Sea: East of Ramandu's Island, this sea—unlike a normal sea, with briny water—has clear and sweet-tasting water that sustains the sailors on the *Dawn Treader*. It is occupied by the Sea People, who hunt in packs, using "fierce fish" on their wrists, much like a falconers with birds of prey.

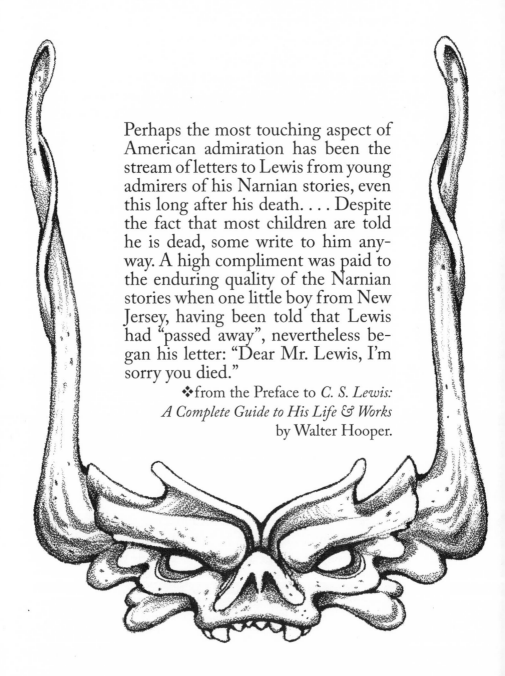

Perhaps the most touching aspect of American admiration has been the stream of letters to Lewis from young admirers of his Narnian stories, even this long after his death. . . . Despite the fact that most children are told he is dead, some write to him anyway. A high compliment was paid to the enduring quality of the Narnian stories when one little boy from New Jersey, having been told that Lewis had "passed away", nevertheless began his letter: "Dear Mr. Lewis, I'm sorry you died."

❖from the Preface to *C. S. Lewis: A Complete Guide to His Life & Works* by Walter Hooper.

THE SILVER CHAIR

It was a dull autumn day and Jill Pole was crying behind the gym.

She was crying because they had been bullying her. This is not going to be a school story, so I shall say as little as possible about Jill's school, which is not a pleasant subject.

❖ the opening paragraphs to *The Silver Chair*

Background

ACCORDING TO KATHRYN LINDSKOOG, alternate titles for this book included *The Wild Waste Lands*, *Night under Narnia*, *Gnomes under Narnia*, and *News under Narnia*.

The principal characters in this sequel to *The Voyage of the Dawn Treader* are Jill Pole and Eustace Clarence Scrubb, who are enrolled at a school called Experiment House, where the traditional educational process is subverted. At this school, children are given too free a rein—a reign of terror. "These people," wrote Lewis, "had the idea that boys and girls should be allowed to do what they liked. And unfortunately what ten or fifteen of the biggest boys and girls liked best was bullying the others." The heads of Experiment House encouraged their behavior because "they were interesting psychological cases," which meant that the bullying was unending.

One of the students, Jill Pole, is in the shrubbery behind the gym, where she has just finished a crying jag, when Eustace Scrubb comes upon her.

As with the initial meeting between Polly Plummer and Digory Kirke, this meeting between Jill and Eustace is hardly promising, but when Eustace tells her of another place, a better place, a magical place, Jill pays rapt attention. Anyplace, she realizes, is better than this place, where the real horror is what happens behind closed doors when the bullies decide that a student needs correction. As Lewis recounts in this novel, "Eustace gave a shudder. Everyone at Experiment House knew what it was like being 'attended to' by Them."

Not knowing how to enter Narnia, they chant Aslan's name repeatedly, which opens a door to Narnia—just in time, too, since one of their tormentors, Edith Jackle, is in hot pursuit.

But the school, its grounds, and England itself are gone; in their place, a large and colorful forest opens up to the edge of a towering cliff, unimaginably high. The little cottonlike puffballs below turn out to be clouds.

Aslan has brought them to Narnia on a mission: to find, and bring back, Prince Rilian, the son of King Caspian the Tenth, who is now old and needs his son to assume the throne.

But where is Rilian? And will Jill remember the guiding signs? Those, says Aslan, will lead to her to Prince Rilian. And what will Jill and Eustace do if they are beset by strange beasts?

With heart in mouth and with the best of intentions to do exactly as Aslan has directed her, Jill sets off with Eustace on a mission that will either end in the return of Prince Rilian . . . or abject failure.

Jill and Eustace do meet others on the road—some who help, and some who do not. Early on, they meet a strange creature named Puddleglum, a Marsh-wiggle from the Eastern Marshes of Narnia. Tall and looking very much like a person who would live in a marsh (green-gray hair, muddy complexion, and solemn of expression), he is quick to always see disaster right around the corner. Can they—or should they—trust him?

Or should they trust the beautiful maiden on a horse, accompanied by a black knight whose visor is down, whom they meet on the road? Knowing they seek refuge from the forbidding terrain, she tells them that she is of the Green Kirtle and directs them to the nearest sanctuary, the House of Harfang, the Gentle Giants. Jill, Eustace, and Puddleglum will be warmly greeted there, she promises, and all they have to do is give the giants her name and tell them that she is sending them two children for their Autumn Feast. The Gentle Giants, she assures them, would not turn them away. And, indeed, they do not. The giants seem kindhearted, wanting only to serve them.

But things are not always what they seem, and the trio are far from familiar (and safe) territory as they doggedly pursue their mission to find Prince Rilian at all costs—a mission that has been in jeopardy ever since they left Aslan on the precipice.

Possibly because of its bleakness—the long journey undertaken by Jill and Eustace and their grim encounters, especially underground—Lewis remarked that this was the least popular of the Narnia books.

This is the last book in the Prince Caspian trilogy.

Main Characters

Jill Pole: A brave and resourceful girl who is tasked by Aslan to help Eustace Scrubb on a mission to find Prince Rilian. This is her first excursion into Narnia.

Eustace Scrubb: A much-changed person in the aftermath of his experiences recounted in *The Voyage of the* Dawn Treader, he proves his mettle and, in his second excursion to Narnia, learns a lot he didn't know about Narnia and about himself as well.

Prince Rilian: The son of Prince Caspian the Tenth, he is the lost prince of Narnia, the heir to the throne, and is the subject of the search undertaken by Jill Pole and Eustace Scrubb, a mission given to them by Aslan.

Puddleglum: A lugubrious marsh creature that hails from the Eastern Marshes of Narnia, his name is suggestive: *puddle* (to be wet with water) and *glum* (looking or feeling dejected). Unlike those who see a silver lining in every cloud, Puddleglum is the kind who sees, and predicts, nothing but doom and gloom in every situation.

The Queen of the Deep Realm: The ruler of the Underland, a beautiful queen who holds sway over the Earthmen, whom she is marshalling for an attack against those who live aboveground.

The Earthmen: Gnomes pressed into service by the Queen of the Deep Realm, these creatures hail from the Land of Bism, which is deep beneath the earth. The area the gnomes live and work in—the realm of the queen—is called by them the Shallow Lands.

Coin Design for barnes & Noble

The Last Battle

In the last days of Narnia, far up to the west beyond Lantern Waste and close beside the great waterfall, there lived an Ape.

❖ opening paragraph to *The Last Battle*

Background

ACCORDING TO KATHRYN LINDSKOOG, this book's original working titles included *The Last King of Narnia* and *Night Falls on Narnia.*

In a letter in 1962 to a child named Sydney, posthumously published in *C. S. Lewis: Letters to Children,* Lewis explained, "I'm afraid I've said all I had to say about Narnia, and there will be no more of these stories."

Though Lewis did not, as his colleague J. R. R. Tolkien did, rigorously outline, plan, and rewrite the Narnia novels to form an interlocked, coherent whole, all things in Narnia must come to an end, and so they do, in the last chronicle of Narnia.

As you make your way further into this novel, it's clear that the numinous flashes seen in the previous novels foreshadow what is to come in this one. In this novel, we see Aslan in all his glory.

The book begins simply enough on a humorous note. We meet two talking animals: Shift, an aptly named wizened ape, who is too clever for his own good, and his stooge, a good-hearted donkey named Puzzle who does Shift's bidding. Both of them live up to their namesakes. To be shifty is to be deceitful and evasive; and to be puzzled is to be confused, incapable of making sense of something.

Shift is crafty and simply uses the trusting Puzzle for his own ends. As Shift patiently explains: "Now, Puzzle, I understand what needs to be done better than you. You know you're not clever, Puzzle."

Any complaints from Puzzle come to a quick end, as he gamely agrees with Shift, and the one-sided relationship predictably continues in Shift's favor.

One day, though, a curious thing happens: in the Cauldron Pool, Shift spies the skin of a lion. Knowing how physically uncomfortable it would be for him to retrieve it, he badgers a reluctant Puzzle to retrieve it for him, no matter what the risk.

Puzzle, of course, puts up token resistance, rightly pointing out that Shift can grab things easier than he can, but the shifty ape easily deflects the argument by making Puzzle feel guilty even for asking; doesn't everyone, even a dumb donkey, know that apes have weak chests and could easily catch a cold in the water?

Making a move to enter the water, Shift knows full well that Puzzle will protest and plead, and so he does. Shift deliberately does this to inflict guilt on Puzzle—one of the many ways Shift exerts control over the unsuspecting donkey.

Puzzle goes into the swirling waters and, after a good deal of physical distress, manages to grab the skin with his teeth and drag it out of the water.

Shift, of course, has a crafty plan—one that requires drafting the puzzled donkey against his will. The plan is to outfit Puzzle in the skin and claim he is Aslan, a plan that allows Shift to have exclusive access to "Aslan" and be his mouthpiece as well.

Seen only occasionally, at night, and under very controlled circumstances, for only a few moments, Puzzle passes for Aslan, and all the talking animals gape in wonder at the turn of events. They know Aslan to be good and kind, so why is it that he is suddenly—according to Shift—angry and cruel, and now wants the forests with its living dryads (tree spirits) denuded and the talking animals sent off into slavery to the harsh men of the south, the Calormen?

In all of this, Puzzle is the victim, of course, but in his new guise—one that wouldn't hold up under close examination—Shift, in alliance with the Calormen, wants to use him to upset the balance of power in Narnia. All the evil parties, however, have their own, cleverly hidden agendas.

All of this can be read in the stars, if one is a centaur and can decipher the celestial meanings. The centaur Roonwit tells King Tirian that, despite the common belief that Aslan has returned, the stars tell of no such coming. Indeed, the stars tell a far different story. Aslan has not come, and evil times are ahead. The stars, Roonwit reminds the king, do not lie, though mortals often do.

Roonwit speaks the truth, for war is inevitable. The Calormen march north to attack King Tirian's forces, and those in Narnia choose which side they will fight on. It will be the last battle in Narnia, and King Tirian will need all the help he can get, especially when Shift and the Calormen invoke the false god of the Calormenes—a false god that, bidden by his people, comes forth, with disastrous consequences.

Jill Pole and Eustace Scrubb come to King Tirian's aid after they are transported to Narnia by his plea for help. "Children! Children! Friends of Narnia! Quick. Come to me. Across the worlds I call you. . . ."

And so the stage is set. The king of the Calormen has sent his massive army to do battle with King Tirian's forces, and the fate of Narnia hangs in the balance.

With this last novel about Narnia, all things come to an end. In its closing chapters, we witness the power and the everlasting beauty of Aslan, who makes his final appearance. We see long-forgotten characters that we met in the earlier books. And we learn the fates of those whom we saw move on to the other side, beyond the world of the living.

We see Lewis's vision of Narnia in all its glory. We see, finally, the everlasting light.

Note: This book won the Carnegie Medal for Children's Literature.

Main Characters

Shift: An old ape who lusts for power over the talking animals, he raises a false god—dressing a donkey in a lion's skin—and demands that all the talking animals pay homage and obey his orders, which he as the mouthpiece of "Aslan" dispenses.

A cagey old animal, Shift takes advantage of Puzzle, a donkey. In the end, it is Shift and not Puzzle who is, in fact, the real ass.

Puzzle: A kindhearted donkey who, flattered that the clever Shift will allow him in his company, does his bidding, not knowing that Shift is merely using him for his own purposes—even to the point of blasphemy, by raising Puzzle high as a false god to subjugate the talking animals in Narnia.

Tash: A false god, he is the demon god of the Calormenes, who unwittingly (and unwisely) call to him. To their great surprise (and horror), Tash comes.

Tash the Destroyer lives up to his name, striking fear in the hearts of those who see him. The Calormenes were foolish to invoke him, because when they realize what they unwisely beckoned—a tall and monstrous man-like creature with a large beak and four arms—they wish he had never come. But Tash is now in Narnia, an evil god summoned by evil men.

Rishda Tarkaan: The captain of the Calormenes, he allies himself with Shift in a power play against King Tirian's forces, but it's only a temporary alliance. Captain Tarkaan wants to use

Shift for his own purpose, just as Shift wants to use the false Aslan for his own purpose. In the end, Captain Tarkaan doesn't get what he wishes, but does get what he deserves.

Tashlan: Shift uses the fear of Tashlan, a named coined by combining Tash (the demon god of the Calormenes) with Aslan (the true god of Narnia), to cow the other talking beasts into submission.

Ginger the Cat: A talking animal, Ginger is exceptionally sly, and is in collusion with Captain Tarkaan, as both pretend to be in an alliance with Shift, but it's only a temporary one. Together, Ginger and Captain Tarkaan conspire to outwit Shift, whom they intend to dethrone.

In a carefully choreographed play, Ginger the Cat "volunteers" to enter the shed to meet Tashlan, but what Ginger meets in the shed is something altogether unexpected—a catastrophe. After seeing the shed's frightful occupant, Ginger is struck speechless and emerges from the shed at top speed, runs up the nearest tree, and is never seen (or heard) again.

COIN DESIGN FOR BARNES & NOBLE

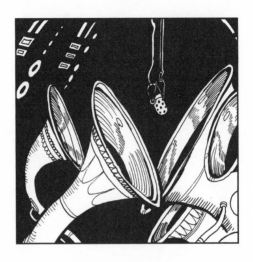

THE CHRONICLES OF NARNIA:
A DRAMATIZATION

The Chronicles of Narnia by C. S. Lewis, dramatized by Focus on the Family Radio Theater on 19 CDs with a running time of 22 hours; $49.97.

IT WAS A TIME when television, computers, the Internet, and cell phones didn't exist. It was 1938, and the majority of Americans owned a radio from which they got their fix of news and entertainment. But on a fateful Halloween night, they got a little of both ... or so they thought.

After adapting popular fiction such as *Dracula* and *The Count of Monte Cristo*, Orson Welles's Mercury Theater decided to present H. G. Wells's *The War of the Worlds* with a unique twist. Instead of presenting it as a fictional story, they deliberately presented it as if it was an actual event, with normal programming interrupted by news bulletins and government announcements.

Listeners who thought they were listening to "Ramon

Raquello and his orchestra" were in fact listening to Welles's aural treat, a Halloween trick. By harnessing the suggestive power of radio to dramatize events, Orson Welles fooled listeners into thinking that the world was being invaded by Martians who had landed in Grover's Hill, New Jersey, and were headed to New York City.

Afterward, everyone had a good laugh, but at the time, it was no laughing matter: a panicked public flooded the local police stations with phone calls, desperately wanting more information about the attack and how to protect themselves.

The Halloween prank underscored the power of the radio dramatization, which draws its potency from its ability to spark the listener's imagination.

Radio Theater produced a dramatization of all seven Narnia novels, recorded on nineteen CDs. Hosted and introduced by Lewis's stepson, Douglas Gresham, the dramatization was appropriately recorded with an all-English cast, including Paul Scofield, David Suchet, and Ron Moody.

The advantage of a radio dramatization over a movie is that a movie's strong visual impact, its cast, its scenery—in short, its visual storytelling—will imprint over your imagination, whereas a good dramatization gives your imagination full play: you decide what the characters and the scenery in Narnia look like.

Though the Disney film of *The Lion, the Witch and the Wardrobe* will undoubtedly exert a powerful influence over viewers' imaginations, the film series is a long way from completion. So far, two additional films have been budgeted—the early response from fans and critics alike all but assure that the first will be a monster hit—but why wait to experience the remaining Narnian tales when you can experience all of them aurally right now? For those who can't wait for the films, this audio recording offers wonderful, interpretive performances by all its cast members.

"THE CHRONICLES OF NARNIA" ON AUDIO CD

The Chronicles of Narnia by C. S. Lewis, Harper Audio, enhanced CD format with unabridged recordings, 31 CDs, with a running time of 31 hours; $75.

The Magician's Nephew, read by Kenneth Branagh (four CDs).

The Lion, the Witch and the Wardrobe, read by Michael York (four CDs).

The Horse and His Boy, read by Alex Jennings (four CDs).

Prince Caspian, read by Lynn Redgrave (four CDs).

The Voyage of the Dawn Treader, read by Derek Jacobi (five CDs).

The Silver Chair, read by Jeremy Northam (five CDs).

The Last Battle, read by Patrick Stewart (five CDs).

Until recently, the unabridged audiobook of *The Chronicles of Narnia* was limited to an aural presentation. With this new edition, however, the color artwork by Pauline Baynes can be viewed when the CD is put into a computer, and its links will take you to Web sites on the World Wide Web, hence its "Enhanced" CD format. (Note: the links are minimal: one takes you to the publisher's Web site and the other takes you to the official movie Web site, www.narnia.com).

This set of CDs is beautifully packaged in a cardboard slipcase with seven inserts, one for each book in the series. Each insert is illustrated in color with Pauline Baynes's charming illustrations.

The real bonus of this set is that it has multiple readers, offering different aural flavors. My personal favorite is Patrick Stewart, who is best known for his work on *Star Trek* as Captain Jean-Luc Picard. Those who are more familiar with him know that he is renowned for his one-man dramatization on stage of *A Christmas Carol* by Charles Dickens. He has also read the book in an abridged edition for an audio recording and, in 1999, starred in a telecast of Dickens's classic.

Stewart throws himself into the reading with gusto. It is apparent that he is not only enjoying himself, but takes special pains to provide an exacting performance: every word, each intonation, hits just the right note. He is meticulous in his reading and, when the occasion requires, becomes properly animated when dramatizing some of the more hilarious scenes, especially those involving Ginger the Cat.

To read the book is an experience unto itself; to hear a professional actor like Stewart read the book to you is a delight, a joy, and an entirely different experience, but one that you will welcome. I guarantee you will agree Stewart is the cat's meow.

THE CHRONICLES OF NARNIA: THE BBC PRODUCTIONS

PACKAGED FOR RERELEASE in 2005, this three-disc set includes: *The Lion, the Witch and the Wardrobe* (169 minutes); *Prince Caspian & the Voyage of the* Dawn Treader (168 minutes); and *The Silver Chair* (168 minutes). Running time, approximately nine hours. Digitally remastered, all have monaural sound.

Each disc includes supplementary material.

The Lion, the Witch and the Wardrobe offers an interactive game (a trivia challenge), a brief profile of Lewis and the restoration of his house (The Kilns) that aired on the BBC, a recipe for Turkish delight, and a gallery of still images.

Prince Caspian & the Voyage of the Dawn Treader offers an interactive game (a trivia challenge) and a gallery of still images.

The Silver Chair offers an interactive game (a trivia challenge) and a gallery of still images.

No one should mistake the BBC production of *The Lion, the Witch and the Wardrobe* for the Disney version, since the two are worlds apart. Judging from the brief, tantalizing trailer currently available online (www.narnia.com), the Disney film adaptation is magical indeed. With a budget big enough to bring Lewis's vision to the screen, and with special effects that make the otherworldly inhabitants of Narnia come alive in a realistic fashion, Disney's will be the one fans will likely remember and forever love.

In the interim, though, fans who want their Narnia fix may find it with this boxed set of the first four Narnia books. Though the BBC adaptations have their advocates, today's moviegoing audience will likely find the pacing a bit slow, the costuming (notably the lion) unconvincing, and the viewing experience a bit lackluster. However, some of the individual performances are certainly worth watching, notably the over-the-top White Witch.

Disc 1: *The Lion, the Witch and the Wardrobe*
1. Away to the Countryside
2. Lucy Looks into a Wardrobe
3. What Lucy Finds
4. Very Bad Faun
5. Edmund and the Wardrobe
6. Turkish Delight
7. The Prophecy
8. On This Side of the Door
9. Into the Forest
10. A Day with the Beavers
11. After Dinner
12. Edmund's Journey
13. In the Witch's House
14. The Spell Begins to Break
15. Aslan Is Near
16. Peter's First Battle
17. Edmund Is Rescued
18. Deep Magic

19. Preparing for Battle
20. Triumph of the Witch
21. Deeper Magic
22. Battle Lines Are Formed
23. The Statues
24. The White Witch Attacks
25. After the Battle
26. Once a King in Narnia

Disc 2: *Prince Caspian & The Voyage of the* Dawn Treader
Prince Caspian
1. The Dwarf
2. Caspian's Adventure
3. People in Hiding
4. Narnia in Danger
5. What Lucy Saw
6. Sorcery and Vengeance
7. The High King in Command
8. The Picture in the Bedroom

The Voyage of the Dawn Treader
1. On Board
2. The Lone Islands
3. Caspian
4. The Storm
5. The Aftermath
6. The Adventures of Eustace
7. How the Adventure Ended
8. A Narrow Escape
9. Another Narrow Escape
10. Island of the Voices
11. The Magician's Book
12. Dufflepuds Made Happy
13. Dark Island

14. Three Sleepers
15. Beginning of the End
16. Wonders of the Last Sea
17. The Very End
18. A Door in the Air

Disc 3: *The Silver Chair*
1. The Unlocked Door
2. Jill's Task
3. Four Signs
4. The Sailing of the King
5. A Parliament of Owls
6. The Story of the Lost Prince
7. Puddleglum
8. Eel Stew
9. An Encounter with Giants
10. She of the Green Kirtle
11. Hill of the Strange Trenches
12. House of Harfang
13. Writing on a Stone
14. Something Worth Knowing
15. Man Stew
16. Warden of the Underworld
17. Travels without the Sun
18. Black Knight
19. Evil Enchantment
20. The Last Sign
21. The Queen of Underland
22. The Slaying of the Queen
23. Underland Without the Queen
24. The Object of His Voyage
25. The New King of Narnia
26. Aslan's Country

Perspectives

Karin Snelson for amazon.com: "Youngsters expecting special effects like those found in *The Lord of the Rings* or *Harry Potter and the Sorcerer's Stone* may miss the subtler charms of these sweet but rather homespun productions, with humans dressed as woodland creatures and patched-in animation. . . . But those who want a refresher course in all things Narnia will be thrilled to see these well-loved fantasies come to life. . . ."

Jonathan Tissue on amazon.com: "I realized that all of this film's weaknesses were simply the result of a very low budget. The acting, scenery, and the truthfulness to the book were all great. They simply could not have possibly made these films any better with the amount of resources that they were allotted. So let's give credit where credit is due."

"Damarian Dreamer" on amazon.com: "I first saw these movies on Public TV, PBS, when I was maybe four or five years old, and my mom had the foresight to record them to videotape for me. . . . Even at 20 years old, I still like to revisit my childhood for a time and I hope to share them with my children when the time comes, that being when I become a mom."

Anyone for Turkish Delight?

In *The Lion, the Witch and the Wardrobe*, Edmund Pevensie becomes addicted—and who can blame him—to Turkish delight. He really can't help himself, for the candy has been enchanted by the White Witch. Among many of the false promises she makes, Edmund Pevensie is especially interested in the unending supply of Turkish delight she has in her castle. All he has to do, she tells him, is to bring his other three siblings to her, and he can eat to his heart's content.

For those who prefer unadulterated (that is, nonenchanted) Turkish delight, there are numerous recipes for it posted on the World Wide Web; use your favorite search engine to locate a recipe with the appropriate measurements (U.S. or metric).

If you're not a cook, Bayco Confectionery offers Turkish delight for sale:

Bayco Confectionery has always been associated with quality products. In accordance with a traditional Turkish recipe passed down through generations, each batch of Turkish Delight is precisely and caringly handcrafted to create a unique product, delicately flavored and lightly scented. Pure natural sugar, mountain fresh British Columbian water and natural fruit flavors are some of the ingredients used to create our many varieties of Turkish Delight. We carry a variety of nut-based natural Turkish Delight (pistachio, almond, hazelnut and walnut). Our pistachio Turkish Delight is by far our most popular nut-based product. Only the highest quality imported pistachios, lightly roasted to bring out their full flavor, and finely desiccated coconut are used to create this very popular line. Our assorted and fruit Turkish Delights are subtly flavored with natural fruit and herbal extracts of apple, apricot, coconut, bergamot, banana, blueberry, lemon, lime, maple, mint, orange, peach, pineapple, raspberry, rose, strawberry, sour cherry and vanilla. Our products are also available in mastic (gum arabic), natural (plain) and chocolate. We offer our Turkish Delight in an assortment of quantities and packaging. Assorted bulk and gift packages will include at least four of the above-mentioned flavors. We also offer a variety of attractive shrink-wrapped gift packages.

To order, contact Bayco Confectionery.
Mail: PO Box 173, Blaine, WA 98231-0173.
Phone: (604) 716-0909
Phone/Fax: (604) 881-2440
e-mail: see "Contact Us" on the Web site
Web site: www.turkish-delight.com

PART 3: THE FILM WORLD OF NARNIA

Bringing "The Chronicles of Narnia" to the Screen

I . . . found C. S. Lewis's writings—all of his books—a wealth of fantasy worlds I could celebrate myself. I read *The Magician's Nephew* first—most people enter Narnia through *The Lion, the Witch and the Wardrobe*. *The Horse and His Boy* is my favorite. To me, that book has an intimacy that none of the others have, while still painting this vast landscape of worlds and turmoil. It was [necessary] to really understand the mythology through all the books to bring reality to the book we were making. *Voyage of the* Dawn Treader explores the world of Narnia more thoroughly than any of the others, and that's where we were able to pick up so many of our notations on cultural references. It was a delight, when we entered Narnia, to discover that much of the team had an incredible amount of knowledge in the world of Narnia, just due to the fact that it was so heavily read in this country.

❖Richard Taylor interviewed
by www.filmforce.ign.com

IT ONLY TOOK ONE MAN a modest investment of time, paper, and ink to write the first of seven novels chronicling Narnia, but it will take a small army to bring it to life, and at an estimated cost of $150 million. It's a kingly sum for any movie, much less a fantasy film, but the unexpected box office success of *The Lord of the Rings* forever changed Hollywood's perception of what's bankable and what's not.

Disney's underwhelming track record with fantasy films was cited as the principal reason why its executives didn't want to invest any more money in what they saw as an increasingly expensive and problematic film. Consequently, Disney bailed and New Line Cinema took over *The Lord of the Rings*—a critical and financial success, to Disney's chagrin.

What Disney didn't realize—despite then-CEO Michael Eisner's mantra that story is everything—is that the moviegoing public isn't interested in fantasy per se, but it craves a well-told tale, which is what *The Lord of the Rings* delivered.

After a clean sweep of the Academy Awards in 2003, *The Return of the King* made it unmistakably clear that good fantasy was here to stay. Winning in every category in which it was nominated, *The Return of the King* reaped eleven Oscars, including best picture of the year. In his acceptance speech, director Peter Jackson echoed the thoughts of millions of fantasy fans with his heartfelt comments: "I'm so honored and relieved that the academy and the members of the academy that have supported us have seen past the trolls and the wizards and the hobbits in recognizing fantasy this year."

The trappings of fantasy aside, the box office success of *The Return of the King*, which brought in a billion dollars worldwide, sent shock waves through Hollywood, and studio executives frantically searched for more fantasy.

As Viggo Mortensen (Aragorn from *The Lord of the Rings*) observed in the wake of the films' success, moviegoers can expect a mix of bad fantasy and good fantasy films in the long term. The good films will include Warner Bros.' Harry Potter film adaptations (*Harry Potter and the Goblet of Fire* in November 2005); New Line Cinema's *His Dark Materials: The Golden Compass*, the first in a trilogy based on the books by British author Philip Pullman, slated to hit movie screens in 2007; and, in between both of them, the movie version of the first published book in the Chronicles of Narnia, *The Lion, the Witch and the Wardrobe*.

Hoping for an ongoing film franchise on the order of *The Lord of the Rings*, Walden Media, in partnership with Disney, plans to issue all seven of the Narnia novels, though its ad slogan suggests even more films to come, should the initial seven prove successful: "There are a thousand stories in the land of Narnia. . . . The first is about to be told."

Whether or not Narnia will become as well known as Middle-earth remains to be seen. But make no mistake: the considerable investment of time, money, and effort to bring Narnia to the screen is a calculated risk that will pay off. At the heart of *The Lion, the Witch and the Wardrobe* is a story that has stood the test of time since 1950, religiously read by devotees of fantasy and Christian fiction, with a built-in audience numbering in the tens of millions.

As with any major motion picture, the lion's share of what had to be done to bring the movie to the public's attention began in earnest well before the film's release. In the case of *The Lion, the Witch and the Wardrobe*, the eagerly anticipated trailer was released worldwide in May 2005 on the online Web site Moviefone. Says film director Andrew Adamson, "I'm pleased to present to you the online world premiere of our teaser trailer only on Moviefone."

The word teaser is accurate. Running only two minutes, it's simply a taste of what is to come in the final movie, which will run nearly three hours.

But it is enough. With its inspiring soundtrack, gorgeous cinematography, and special effects, it transfixes the viewer, making the unbelievable believable. There is a wondrous world beyond the wardrobe, past the lamppost in the region of Narnia called Lantern Waste.

The trailer opens with the sound of a train roaring by. The train clears the platform and we see four children: Peter, Susan, Edmund, and Lucy Pevensie, who await the arrival of Mrs. Macready, a stern-looking woman who takes them back to the Professor's house out in the country. The kids don't know what to expect—they were evacuated from London during World War II because of Hitler's bombing campaign against the city. They have no inkling that their lives will irrevocably change, for soon they will enter a brave, new world—Narnia.

When the children arrive at the house, Mrs. Macready lays down the rules. The Professor, she states firmly, is unaccustomed to children, so please observe the following: *no* shouting, *no* running, *no* sliding on the banisters, *no* touching of the historical artifacts, and, above all, there will be *no disturbing the professor!*

The children understand. In fact, since they see only his shadow under doors, he's a mysterious figure. But they are reconciled to staying at his house for the long term—at least until it's safe to return to London.

Playing a game of hide-and-seek, the children scatter throughout the house; Lucy opens a door that leads to an empty room, dominated by a cloth-covered object. Light coming in through the windows gives the object an otherworldly glow. There is something magical about the object, and the curious child steps forward. Pulling the cloth down, she reveals the ornate wardrobe with its elaborately carved panels towering above her. She stares in childlike wonder. She gingerly reaches out to touch the wardrobe and, wanting to see what's within, pulls open the door, and a light shines forth.

What little Lucy doesn't know is that she will soon enter Narnia. Among the Pevensie children, it is the youngest, Lucy, who will lead the way for the rest of them.

In the next scene, we see all four Pevensie children surrounded by a snowy landscape. A lamppost beckons—a beacon of light. "Impossible!" says Susan, who can't believe what she sees. They are on a stone bridge covered with snow and gaze out at Narnia in all its unnatural winter glory—a perpetual condition created by the aptly named White Witch, who has covered Narnia in ice and snow. It will always be winter but never Christmas in Narnia, as Lewis reminds us in the novel itself, until Aslan bounds onto the scene.

We then see snippets of the movie: leaping merpeople, a colorful medieval tent with wondrous creatures (including a centaur) surrounding it, and the Pevensie children bowing before and swearing allegiance to Aslan, who is framed in a large window, with the sun behind him.

Flashes of light, flashes of darkness.

We see a night scene in which the White Witch is preparing a sacrifice on the Stone Table, surrounded by her evil minions, creatures of darkness.

We see the four Pevensie children in full regalia, standing in front of their respective thrones. They are the predestined rulers of Narnia, the Sons of Adam and the Daughters of Eve.

We see a massive army gathering in front of snow-capped mountains: the forces of good, represented by Aslan and his followers, who prepare to do battle against the White Witch and her evil hench-creatures.

The forces of good surge forward, shouting battle cries, and clash with the forces of evil. Mayhem ensues. The battle is joined, but to what end?

The tantalizing trailer concludes with Aslan standing on a verdant mountaintop, roaring loudly for all of Narnia to hear. The camera pulls back and we see the wintry landscape that surrounds him.

If the movie lives up to the promise of the trailer, moviegoers are in for a visual treat. The kind of movie that demands to be seen on a large screen, this is what moviemaking is all about: the spectacle, the grandeur, and the scope of an imaginative world brought to larger than life.

The accompanying soundtrack is evocative and moving, memorable and inspiring, just as the movie promises to be. The trailer has done its job: we are hooked and we want more. Like Lucy Pevensie, we, too, want to explore Narnia, but unlike her, we must patiently wait until December 9, 2005.

Mark your calendars, for this is a movie that should not be missed.

Film Credits

Andrew Adamson, Director

Stephen Barton, Harry Gregson-Williams, Amy Lee, *Original Music*

Donald McAlpine, *Cinematography*

Jim May and *Sim Evan-Jones*, *Film Editing*

Sameer Bhardwaj, Pippa Hall, Liz Mullane, Gail Stevens, *Casting*

Roger Ford, *Production Design*

Jules Cook, Ian Gracie, Karen Murphy, Jeffrey Thorp, Art Direction

Kerrie Brown, *Set Decoration*

Isis Mussenden, *Costume Design*

Writing Credits

C. S. Lewis, on whose novel the movie is based

Andrew Adamson, Christopher Markus, Stephen McFeely, and *Ann Peacock*, screenplay

Cast

Ben Barrington as Centaur #2

Jim Broadbent as Professor Digory Kirke

Greg Cooper as Faun #1
James Cosmo as Father Christmas
Shelly Edwards as distraught mother #1
Rupert Everett as the voice of the Fox
Dawn French as the voice of Mrs. Beaver
Felicity Hamill as Hag #3
Elizabeth Hawthorne as Mrs. Macready
Georgie Henley as Lucy Pevensie
Rachael Henley as Lucy Pevensie (adult)
Sam La Hood as Satyr #2
Noah Huntley as Peter Pevensie (adult)
Patrick Kake as Oreius
Skandar Keynes as Edmund Pevensie
Richard King as Faun #2
Sandro Kopp as a Centaur
James McAvoy as Mr. Tumnus (the faun)
Judy McIntosh as Mrs. Pevensie
William Moseley as Peter Pevensie
Liam Neeson as the voice of Aslan
Alina Phelan as Centaur archer
Russell Pickering as Faun #3
Anna Popplewell as Susan Pevensie
Shane Rangi as General Otmin
Allison Sarofim as Chief Battle Dryad
Kiran Shah as Ginarrbrik
Tilda Swinton as Queen Jadis, the White Witch
Julian Timm as an Elf
Stephen Ure as Satyr
Mark Wells as Edmund Pevensie (adult)
Charles Williams as Centaur #3
Sophie Winkleman as Susan Pevensie (adult)

Producers
Andrew Adamson, executive producer
Douglas Gresham, coproducer
Mark Johnson, producer
Perry Moore, executive producer
Philip Steuer, executive producer

How the Lucky Few Already Saw The Film

ONE OF THE ADVANTAGES of living near Hollywood is that if you're lucky, you may get to see a screening of your favorite movies months in advance.

On August 31, 2005, people in La Verne, California, were able to catch a test screening of *The Lion, the Witch and the Wardrobe* at the Edwards theatre. In exchange for the free tickets, selected members of the audience were asked to rate the film afterward; the feedback would be used to fine-tune the final product.

As is usually the case, the test screening was a work in progress. Not all of the special effects had been completed, nor had the film itself been scored, matching scene to music. Even so, the viewers were able to get a sense of the film itself, and the early verdict is in: out of 26 people polled, 21 rated it as excellent, four rated it as very good, and one as good. Not bad!

A reviewer named Bellweather wrote, "As big C. S. Lewis fans, we were amazed and completely thrilled by the movie. I'll avoid plot spoilers for those few who haven't read the books, but suffice it to say, the movie kept quite close to the plot of the book. . . . Overall, this movie more than captures the magic of Lewis's Narnia, and is destined to be a classic film. I will be first in line to see it again when it opens, and it will be a permanent addition to my movie collection. I urge you all to see it on the big screen. Anything less will not do justice to the epic scale of the film."

PERSPECTIVES ON THE FILM VERSION

Andrew Adamson, film director (interviewed by *The New Zealand Herald*): "... [T]he film I am working on at the moment is a book that was very important to me as a child and it's another movie that comes with a lot of expectations because it's a book that a lot of people enjoyed as children. And then going back and reading it as an adult I was surprised by how little was there. C. S. Lewis is someone who paints a picture and lets you imagine the rest. To me it's about making a movie that lives up to my memory of my book rather than specifically the book itself.

"And it needs to live up to everyone else's memories and that is what my challenge is—to make it accessible and real. You read it and it's a 1940s children's book. I want it to feel real and for kids today to actually relate to the children.

"So I've really tried to make the story about a family which is disenfranchised and disempowered in World War II, that on entering Narnia, through their unity as a family become empowered at the end of the story. It's really bringing the humanity of the characters into what is effectively a symbolic story."

From another interview on http://filmforce.ign.com: "This movie is about forgiveness. It's about the kids' forgiveness of each other, it's about Aslan's forgiveness of Edmund. That's an important theme for the current times. So much of the world's situations exist because of a lack of forgiveness. Feuds go on for thousands of years because nobody forgives and moves on. The themes are universal and still very relevant."

Douglas Gresham (C. S. Lewis's stepson), interviewed by www.narniaweb.com: "One of our producers on set one day was introducing me to someone who asked, 'What does he do on this project?' His reply was 'He's to blame.' (laughs) Actually, I am responsible for consultation on all aspects of the production as a sort of in-house Narnia expert. This extends to all spin-off materials, like toys, games, books and so forth. I work with the games guys from the companies contracted to Buena Vista, the merchandising guys from Disney, the publishing teams at Harper-Collins, and I represent the C. S. Lewis Company as its Creative and Artistic Director. Making the movie has been a dearly held ambition and project for me for about thirty years (my children remember me dreaming, scheming, planning, and talking about it all their lives), so every aspect of it is important to me. I suppose I represent Jack [C. S. Lewis] himself as a sort of creative ambassador. The aim of this is to use my abilities, knowledge and experience to make this movie as good as we can possibly make it."

Noah Huntley in the role of King Peter the Magnificent (interviewed on Narniafans.com): "In order to embrace the whole film and therefore place your own part within it, it is interesting to see the work William [Moseley] and the others had done. However, in the end, our sequences were very brief in order to keep to the main story. Really, as far as this first film goes, we show how time operates in Narnia, with many years passing when only seconds or minutes pass in our own world. We also set up the older characters for the future stories. As the high Kings and Queens of Narnia, we are glimpsed as the product of the four children's noble, courageous and compassionate virtues."

Perry Moore, producer (interviewed by Devin Faraci in "The Coverage of Narnia" for http://chud.com): "I went after the rights for Chronicles of Narnia before *Lord of the Rings* and before the Harry Potter films came out. I went after the rights because it was an amazing story and an amazing book from my childhood. I knew I'd have to address this question with the directors or writers or other producers I would have to hire for this movie, so I had an answer prepared: It's a wonderful, great messiah story, not unlike *Star Wars*, not unlike *The Matrix*. If you want to see something more in it, we're doing a movie that's a faithful adaptation of the book, that's there for the people who want to see it. But we're making a movie for everyone, because that book and that story are for everyone. It's not for one group, it's for everyone. And I think we really pull it off."

William Moseley in the role of Peter Pevensie (interviewed by Edward Douglas on the Web site www.comingsoon.net): "We shot seven months in New Zealand and then we shot for two weeks in Prague. It was a life-changing experience. New Zealand is an amazing setting for such an amazing film. I feel like a big city like Los Angeles or London or New York just wouldn't have been right for such a film like that. It almost needs to be in its element. It's a free story about free things, and it needs to be in a free place, and I'm so glad we shot it in New Zealand. I think it was just right."

Anna Popplewell in the role of Susan Pevensie (http://filmforce. ign.com, interviewed by Jeff Otto): "Well, I think everyone was kind of surprised at the idea of Andrew [Adamson] on *The Lion, the Witch and the Wardrobe* because he had a background in animation. The thing is, Andrew's so wonderful with people. He's not only a genius, he's such a nice man. He really knew how to relate to all of us as individuals. It wasn't 'the kids,' he communicated to all of us in different ways appropriately. He's just a brilliant director, really."

Tilda Swinton (in the role of the White Witch), interviewed by Paul Fischer in "The Witch, the Angel, and the Mum: The Many Sides to Tilda Swinton" at the Sundance Film Festival: "I'm really convinced that it will be exactly what it should be, which is a classical, very cinematic adaptation of that book. It's got a really

3D, Technicolor, *Wizard of Oz* feel about it and one of the things that I think is very radical about what [film director] Andrew has done, is he is not interested in special effects anymore so everything's real, so you have real creatures. In other words, you don't have, as in *The Lord of the Rings*, 500 extras that are doubled up to make 7,000, but actually have all of those people in all of those suits, being all of those mythical creatures. It was really good fun, and I really, really love New Zealand."

From http://filmforce.ign.com: "I think the world is divided between those who read the Chronicles of Narnia and those who didn't; or had it read to them. But those were the days before Disney's marketing machine got a hold of Narnia, you see. It's not like *Harry Potter* and *Lord of the Rings* now, which are pushed down everybody's throats. In those days, people kind of discovered it. Let's hope children will still be able to discover it. It's about a children's world. *Lord of the Rings* isn't, really. I think the real question, and I speak as the mother of two six-year-olds, the real question is, 'What do the parents want to read?' And it's lovely to read the Narnia books to children. I'm not taken to the idea of reading *The Lord of the Rings* to my children. I'd be interested to know if most people discovered *The Lord of the Rings* by reading it themselves or whether people read it to them."

Richard Taylor (director, Weta Workshop), interviewed by Rebecca Murray at the San Diego Comicon in 2005: "It's a perfect series of books. It's the spirit of C. S. Lewis's writing: the religious analogies, the coming of good beating evil. As corny as it may sound, all of these things had a resonance through the project because Andrew Adamson built a crew, a team, that would carry that methodology, that mentality, into the project. We felt it and we worked and made sure it was strong in Weta Workshop."

In an interview with http://filmforce.ign.com: "The fans of Narnia do not want to see a reinvention of *Lord of the Rings*. It has to be its own unique reality and it's a very special, special world for an audience. They would be desperately unhappy if we had just rehashed anything. So we set about trying to create a whole unique culture and world."

GIVING FORM AND SHAPE
TO NARNIA:
WETA WORKSHOP

BEFORE THE RELEASE of Peter Jackson's *The Lord of the Rings* film adaptation, few knew of the existence of Weta Workshop. Located on the far side of the world, in Wellington, New Zealand, the special effects and design company that now occupies 65,000 square feet of space had its modest beginning in a small apartment owned by Weta cofounders, Richard Taylor and Tania Rodger.

But when *The Fellowship of the Ring* opened in movie theaters worldwide, the movie-going public sat up and paid attention: Weta Workshop was the magic behind the movie. According to a press release announcing that Richard Taylor would be receiving an honorary doctorate from Victoria University in recognition

Richard Taylor, company director of Weta Workshop

of his body of work, the Weta team consisted of 200 employees who produced from scratch more than 48,000 items, including "900 suits of hand-made armour, 2,000 rubber and safety weapons, 100 special, hand-made weapons, and more than 20,000 other items."

What most people never realized was the amount of work that went into making just one piece, let alone the tens of thousands of artifacts needed to convincingly recreate the world of Middle-earth. As Jamie Wilson of Weta Workshop explained:

> The process of creating the individual collectible pieces is a long and arduous one. Drawing on their experience of working on the movies, Weta's design team initially draw up a number of concepts for pieces based on key sequences from the film. These are then extensively reviewed in collaboration with the director and the studios before a number are then selected. From there, the sculptors take over and spend anything from six to

twenty weeks turning two-dimensional drawings into beautiful three-dimensional sculptures. The sculptors refer to the maquettes for the movie as well as the armour, weapons, costume and numerous images taken from the set, to recreate as closely as possible the finished character that will grace the silver screen. Once the sculpt is approved, the piece is then molded and from there master casts are produced. These casts are then tidied up and assembled to create the finished look of the piece. Half the masters are then sent to the painters who spend several days hand painting the casts using photos and the real costumes as reference. Once the mold and paint masters are finished, they are then sent to the factory for reproduction. There they basically go through the same process again, all the finished collectibles being hand assembled and painted. It can take anything up to nine months to go from the initial design to the finished piece ready for sale.

This arduous process led to the creation of a line of *The Lord of the Rings* collectibles designed by Weta in collaboration with Sideshow Toys—a line that included 180 statues, busts, environments, medallions, and limited-edition Giclée prints.

The overwhelming response to the Weta line of Tolkien collectibles prompted Weta to continue producing more movie-related collectibles, including pieces from Peter Jackson's remake of *King Kong* and the first major Lewis film adaptation, *The Chronicles of Narnia: The Lion, the Witch and the Wardrobe.*

In October 2005, the first pieces will be released, followed by a second wave in December 2005, for a total of ten pieces. As with *The Lord of the Rings* line, the Narnia line will be high-quality, limited-edition pieces individually numbered, available through select retailers that cater to the comics and collectibles markets.

With an onslaught of movie tie-in merchandise—similar to that of *The Lord of the Rings*—as licensees all vie for a piece of the merchandising pie, there will be a lot of forgettable products, but it's safe to say that Weta Workshop's collectibles line will be unforgettable. The attention to detail lavished on their sculptures is remarkable; indeed, in my opinion, owning one of these meticulously crafted sculptures is the best way to have a piece of movie magic from *The Lion, the Witch and the Wardrobe*.

My advice: Don't attempt to buy one of everything, but concentrate on the ones you really like. The line will eventually be expanded to include more sculptures inspired by all seven novels, so picking and choosing carefully will allow you to display them, as opposed to keeping them boxed up and out of view for lack of storage space—a problem completists face.

For more information, go to http://www.wetanz.com.

GARY SCULPTING "VENATOSAURUS ATTACK"

Peter Pevensie on a unicorn. Sculpted by Brigitte Wuest. A limited edition of 3,000 pieces, $300.

GREG TOZER SCULPTING SUSAN AND LUCY ON ASLAN.

Lucy and Susan Pevensie on a bounding Aslan. Sculpted by Greg Tozer. A limited edition of 3,000 pieces, $300.

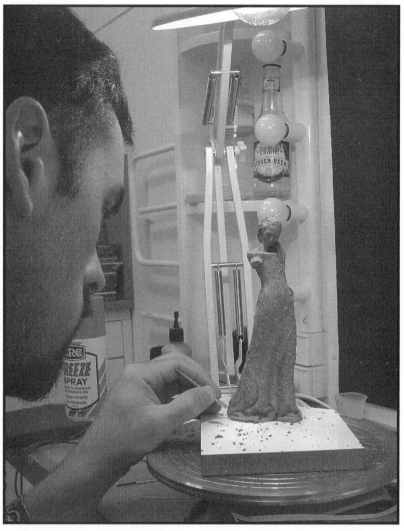

EDEN SMALL SCULPTING THE WHITE WITCH BOOKEND.

The Lion and Witch bookends. Sculpted by Eden Small, Ben Wootten, and John Harvey. A limited edition of 3,500 piec $175.

The Minoboar. Sculpted by Eden Small, Ben Wootten, and John Harvey. A limited edition of 3,000 pieces, $150.

General Otmin. Sculpted by Ryk Fortuna. A limited edition of 3,000 pieces, $150.

Mr. Tumnus. Sculpted by Greg Tozer.
A limited edition of 3,000 pieces, $150.

Oreius. Sculpted by Rob Baldwin, Ryk Fortuna, and John Harvey. A limited edition of 3,000 pieces, $175.

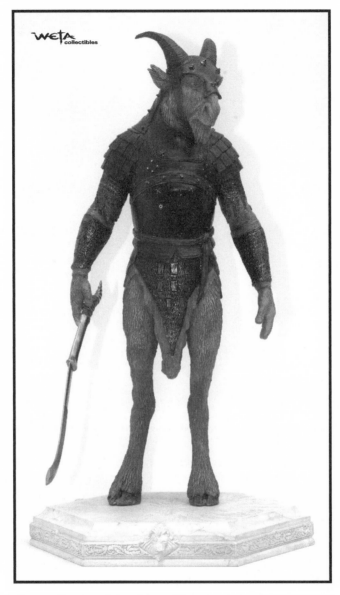

Satyr. Sculpted by Steve Unwin. A limited edition of 3,000 pieces, $150.

CLOSE-UP OF SATYR SCULPTURE.

Ginnabrik and the White Witch. Sculpted by Heather Kilgour and Ryk Fortuna. A limited edition of 3,000 pieces, $180.

THE JEWELRY OF NARNIA: THE BOB SIEMON COLLECTION

Bob Siemon Designs's mission is to create jewelry that gives people an opportunity to share a message of hope. Since C. S. Lewis incorporated the same message in this epic tale of good overcoming evil, the decision to seek a license to create jewelry based on the story was simple. The combination of deep symbolism and fine jewelry really creates a timeless treasure. This collection gives people a lasting impression of the story as well as a way to carry it with them well after they have read Lewis's books or seen the movie.

❖ statement from Bob Siemon Designs

The Product Line

Leaf Pendant ($42). In sterling silver with an 18-inch matching light chain, this pendant symbolizes the rebirth of Narnia after the curse of the White Witch is lifted: no more winter, but spring in all its lush beauty. On the back are the words "Goodness Triumphs."

Lamppost Pendant ($42). An iconic symbol of Narnia, in sterling silver with an 18-inch matching light chain. Suggesting the light from home that beckons to us, the lamppost is the permanent beacon in Western Narnia that shows the Pevensie children the way back to the wardrobe.

Two-Tone Shield Pendant ($58). In sterling silver, with a 14-karat gold crown, this symbol of Aslan represents his kingship over Narnia and his omnipresence, always available to lend a helping paw when the Pevensie children and the others from Earth call out for his aid. On the back of the pendant are the words "Wrong will be right when Aslan comes in sight."

Vial Pendant ($16.99). In pewter with an 18-inch rhodium-plated light cable chain, this represents the vial given by Father Christmas to Lucy Pevensie in *The Lion, the Witch and the Wardrobe*. In the vial is a liquid that magically cures any wound.

Wardrobe Pendant ($18.99). In pewter with an 18-inch rhodium-plated light cable chain, this is my personal favorite of all the pieces. It is the wardrobe that is the gateway from our world to Narnia. In a larger sense, it's symbolic of the power of imagination.

Aslan Pendant ($14.99). In pewter with an 18-inch light cable chain, this small piece shows a full-figure Aslan.

Narnia Charm Bracelet ($24.99). Each of the eight charms portrays a character who represents a significant moment in the movie. Constructed of pewter, this linked chain is eight inches and has an adjustable lobster clasp. A charming gift!

Future Queen Necklace ($9.99). In pewter with purple glitter epoxy, a small crown with its oval-shaped legend, "Future Queen," hangs from an adjustable purple satin 24-inch cord. A perfect gift for the little princess in your family who aspires to be a queen.

Future Queen Key Ring ($6.99). In pewter with purple glitter epoxy, this is the perfect gift for someone who needs to keep track of the keys to her kingdom.

Future Queen Zipper Pull ($4.99). In pewter with purple glitter epoxy, this can be attached to any zipper that has an open hole or slot.

Pewter Shield Pendant ($9.99). A design of Aslan, in red, this pendant is constructed of pewter and comes with an adjustable, stainless steel curb chain (20–24 inches).

Pewter Shield Key Ring ($6.99). In pewter with a red lion design on the front, the back reads, "Wrong will be right when Aslan comes in sight. At the sound of his roar, sorrows will be no more. When he bares his teeth, winter meets its death; and when he shakes his mane, spring shall come again."

Pewter Shield Zipper Pull ($4.99). In pewter with a red lion design, the back repeats the text of the key ring.

For more information, contact Bob Siemon Designs, 3501 W. Segerstrom Avenue, Santa Ana, CA 92704. Telephone: 1-800-854-8358 or (714) 549-0678. Fax: 1-800-621-3442 or (714) 979-2627. Web: www.bobsiemon.com.

VIAL PENDANT

LEAF PENDANT

Narnian Merchandise

THE FLOOD OF PRODUCTS has already begun hitting the shelves of retailers. Ranging from inexpensive printed bookmarkers and journals to more expensive products, including toy replicas and an electronic games, the chances are good that a lot of these items will find their way under Christmas trees this year.

Bookmarkers

From Barnes and Noble, six designs:
1. Peter Pevensie on a unicorn
2. Susan Pevensie with a drawn bow
3. Edmund Pevensie with sword and shield
4. Lucy Pevensie with a vial
5. Aslan overlooking Cair Paravel
6. The White Witch

Journal

From Antioch Publishing, a journal. On the front cover: a silhouette of Aslan against a gold shield; the front endpaper is decorated with snowflakes and the figure of Aslan; the back endpaper is decorated with a seal surrounded by text ("The Lion, the Witch and the Wardrobe"), and snowflakes.

Toys from Master Replicas

These 1/6th-scale replicas are based on designs by Weta Workshop.

1. Lucy's Gifts: a vial, a sword, and a leather belt from which a scabbard and leather pouch hang. It is packaged in a presentation box. $35.

2. Peter's Gifts: a sword and shield (with red lion design). $35.

3. Susan's Gifts: a horn, a quiver with arrows, and a bow. $35.

4. Peter's Sword: a letter opener. A sword with base (Aslan's head). $39.99.

5. Peter's Sword: a full-size replica. $299.99.

6. White Witch's Wand: a full-size replica. $249.99.

Hasbro Action Figures

1. Cyclops with studded mace.
2. Monotaur.
3. Centaur.

Entertainment Earth Figurines

1. Basic Action Figures Wave 1: Aslan, Centaur, Minotaur, Peter Pevensie, and a Black Dwarf.

2. Basic Plush Wave 1: Aslan, Mr. Beaver, and a Unicorn.

3. Basic Battle Figures Wave 1: Aslan's army, Osrieus's army, Otmin's army, and the White Witch's army.

4. Basic Battle Figures Scale 2, Wave 1: Peter Pevensie, the Unicorn, Edmund Pevensie, Lucy Pevensie, Susan Pevensie, Mr. Tumnus, and Aslan.

5. Basic Battle Figures: Ginarrbrick the Dwarf, Maugrim, Aslan, Edmund Pevensie, the Red Dwarf Fighter, a Griffon, and the White Witch.

Board Games

1. A new version of Stratego based on *The Lion, the Witch and the Wardrobe*.

2. An original game (for two to four players) in which the goal is to reach, with Aslan's help, the lamppost, despite obstacles—wolves and the White Witch.

Electronic

The Chronicles of Narnia is an action role-playing game from

Buena Vista Interactive. It will run on Sony PlayStation, Micro-
soft's Xbox, Game Boy Advance, and Nintendo's GameCube.
(For a preview, go to www.NarniaTheGame.com.)

Music

Because *The Lion, the Witch and the Wardrobe* is being marketed
to the Christian and secular markets, there are three different
music tie-in editions.

1. The official soundtrack will be available in two editions: the
regular edition and the special edition. It is composed by Geof-
frey Burgon.

The special edition will include special packaging, photos
from the film, comprehensive liner notes, and a bonus DVD
with interviews and behind the scenes looks at the making of
the music footage.

2. An album will feature music written especially for children.

3. An album will feature music written especially for the
Christian market, titled *Music Inspired by the Chronicles of Nar-
nia*: Jars of Clay ("Waiting for the World to Fall"), Steven Curtis
Chapman ("Remembering You"), Jeremy Camp ("Open Up Your
Eyes"), Bethany Dillon ("Hero"), Delirious ("Stronger"), Rebec-
ca St. James ("Lion"), Nichole Nordeman ("I Will Believe"), The
David Crowder Band ("Turkish Delight"), Kutless ("More than
It Seems), and Chris Tomlin ("You're the One").

PART 4:
BEYOND
THE WARDROBE

RESOURCES

Books about Narnia and C. S. Lewis

Soon after Peter Jackson's *The Fellowship of the Ring* hit the screens, I was in a Barnes and Noble bookstore, in the fantasy section devoted to Tolkien, when I overheard a teenage girl tell her parents, "There are so many books and I don't know what to buy." As it turned out, she was writing a term paper for school, but was frozen with indecision after seeing the shelves of books by and about Tolkien: the selection proved too intimidating.

New Narnia fans will likely feel the same way. A contemporary of Tolkien, C. S. Lewis was a respected critic, a popularizer of Christianity, and a storyteller. Not surprisingly, there are numerous books about him and his body of work, with more to come. The film release of *The Lion, the Witch and the Wardrobe* will be met in the bookstores with the release of books reexamining every facet of C. S. Lewis's life, beliefs, and published works.

The new Narnia fan has a wealth of reading material from which to choose, ranging from scholarly books published by small houses to full-color, illustrated editions that tie in to the Disney movie.

Note: The easiest way to check other titles of related interest is to go to www.Amazon.com and do a search using the keywords *C. S. Lewis*, *Narnia*, or *The Lion, the Witch and the Wardrobe*.

1. *C. S. Lewis & Narnia for Dummies* by Richard Wagner. $19.95, trade paperback, 364 pages, Wiley Publishing, Inc. I'm sure the publisher will hate the comparison, though I mean it in a complimentary way, but the "Dummies" series is the McDonald's of the book-publishing world. The "Dummies" series offers a time-tested format with a uniform presentation.

More for adults than children, this book is divided into five major sections. (1) C. S. Lewis: Christian Apologist and Storyteller; (2) All Things Narnia: Voyaging to the World of Aslan; (3) Tell Me More Stories: Lewis's Other Novels and Fantasies; (4) Getting Real: Discovering Lewis's Nonfiction; and (5) The Part of Tens, which is a summary of the ten top C. S. Lewis and Narnia resources, the ten top classic Lewis quotes, the ten authors recommended by Lewis, and ten tips for reading Lewis. This book is for adults who want an exhaustive overview of the man and his work.

2. *The C. S. Lewis Encyclopedia: A Complete Guide to His Life, Thought, and Writings* by Colin Duriez; $9.99, laminated hardback, 249 pages, Crossway Books. This cross-indexed "A to Z" encyclopedia covers a lot of ground. A cross section of key events in Lewis's life, relationships, and beliefs, it also provides a detailed explication of his fiction and nonfiction, and entries on key characters found in the Narnia novels. As expected, Duriez—one of the most prominent Lewis scholars—does not disappoint.

3. *C. S. Lewis Letters to Children*, edited by Lyle W. Dorsett and Marjorie Lamp Mead; $9, trade paperback, 120 pages, Simon & Schuster. According to the book's editors, C. S. Lewis received fan mail on a daily basis for over two decades.

That's not surprising, since readers will write to their favorite authors. Also not surprising: most of the letters Lewis received from children were because of his Narnia novels. What is surprising is that, as the editors explain, "Although answering so many letters could be tedious, he responded personally to each one, often writing in longhand with a dip-pen and ink."

This charming collection of letters shows how seriously Lewis took the agreeable task of responding to children, who asked him questions about how to pronounce unfamiliar Narnian words, about whether or not he'd write more books in the series, and about specific characters and their destinies, notably Susan's (". . . perhaps she will get to Aslan's country in the end—in her own way").

4. *C. S. Lewis: A Complete Guide to His Life & Works* by Walter Hooper; $19.95, trade paperback, 940 pages, HarperSanFrancisco. Hooper is the literary adviser to the estate of C. S. Lewis. A reknowned Lewis scholar and editor of *The Collected Letters of C. S. Lewis*, Hooper is the authority on Lewis. Simply put, this is the bible for Lewis. Contents include a biography, a chronology, a bibliography of all of Lewis's writings, a glossary of key ideas, a "What's What" guide to the places and things in Lewis's works, and a guide to each of his works. Intended for the serious student or scholar, this definitive book belongs on the shelf of every Lewis fan who wants to go beyond the wardrobe, so to speak, and explore the rest of the Lewis universe.

5. *The Chronicles of Narnia* by C. S. Lewis, with illustrations in black-and-white by Pauline Baynes; $29.99 in hardback (778 pages), $19.99 in trade paperback (767 pages), HarperCollins. The

movie tie-in edition with the seven novels arranged in chrono-logical order. The hardback adds an essay by Lewis, "On Three Ways of Writing for Children."

A single-volume collection, the hardback is the edition of choice. Bound in sewn signatures, it will hold up under repeated readings, though it is heavy to hold, weighing nearly three pounds.

6. *The Chronicles of Narnia Boxed Set* by C. S. Lewis, with il-lustrations in black-and-white by Pauline Baynes; $45, a boxed set of seven trade paperbacks, HarperTrophy. Each volume is small enough to comfortably hold for extended periods of read-ing, and the set is attractively priced online at under $30. For those reasons, it's the best-selling edition of the Chronicles of Narnia online.

Unfortunately, it's the cheapest—in every sense of the word—edition in print, with coarse pulp paper, and overinking of not only the text but of the art: Pauline Baynes's beautiful line work is obliterated. With blotches and splattering of ink throughout, these are embarrassingly badly printed books. From a production point of view, all the money went into the embossed covers with metallic inks at the expense of the interior pages. But do you buy a book for its cover or its contents? No question, HarperCollins needs to address the production values of this lackluster edition.

7. *Companion to Narnia: A Guide to the Magical World of C. S. Lewis* (Revised and expanded for its 2005 publication) by Paul Ford; $16.95, trade paperback, 529 pages, HarperSanFrancisco. A professor of theology and liturgy at St. John's Seminary in Camarillo, California, Paul Ford has studied, and written about, C. S. Lewis for more than four decades. The founder of the Southern California C. S. Lewis Society, Ford's *Companion to Narnia* is arranged alphabetically, with cross-indexed references from Adam to Zardeenah. Intended to be a supplementary text

to the Chronicles of Narnia, it's so thorough and definitive that when the cast and crew of the film needed a single source of information about Narnia, this was the book they consulted.

8. *The Complete Chronicles of Narnia* by C. S. Lewis, with illustrations in color by Pauline Baynes; $50, hardback, 528 pages, HarperCollins. This collects all seven novels in an oversized edition handsomely illustrated by Baynes, who colored her original black-and-white illustrations to stunning effect. The perfect edition for gift giving.

9. *A Field Guide to Narnia: An Overview of the Life and Work of C. S. Lewis* by Colin Duriez; $13, trade paperback, 240 pages, InterVarsity Press. A useful book for adults and children alike, this is divided into three sections: the creation of Narnia (C. S. Lewis's life, the background to Narnia, its literary qualities); all about Narnia (history and geography plus related writings); and an alphabetical guide from A to Z of its people, places, and things. In short, a handy, tightly focused book on Narnia for newcomers. A British writer who has lectured and written extensively on not only C. S. Lewis but J. R. R. Tolkien as well, Duriez is the author of *Tolkien and C. S. Lewis: The Gift of Friendship*, *The C. S. Lewis Encyclopedia*, and (with David Porter) *The Inklings Handbook*. Highly recommended.

10. *A Guide to the C. S. Lewis Tour in Oxford* by Ron Brind; £12, trade paperback. (Available directly from its author; contact Ron@cslewistours.com.) Ronald A. Brind, who conducts a C. S. Lewis tour of Oxford, has put together this useful book, not only for armchair travelers but also for those who need an accessible guide when touring Oxford.

11. *Journey into Narnia* by Kathryn Lindskoog; $15.95, trade paperback, 227 pages, Hope Publishing House. This is two books

in one. The first part, written in 1957 and published in 1973, was originally titled *The Lion of Judah in Never Never Land: The Theology of C. S. Lewis Expressed in His Fantasies for Children*, which won high praise from Lewis himself: "For one thing, you know my work better than anyone I've met, certainly better than I do myself. . . . But secondly you (alone of the critics I've met) realize the connection or even the unity of all the books—scholarly, fantastic, theological. . . . This wins very high marks indeed."

The second part is "Exploring the Narnian Chronicles," a look at each of the seven books, with background information, biblical parallels, and material especially designed for students and teachers.

The text alone is worth the price of admission, but the addition of—oh, joy, oh rapture!—Tim Kirk's art, which originally appeared in various Mythopoeic Society publications, adds the right touch. From the color cover to the map and spot illustrations, Kirk hits the right notes in pictorial terms. Though Kirk ruefully observed that his early work has now come back to haunt him, the fact remains that these timeless illustrations are not so much haunting as they are memorable.

12. *The Land of Narnia* by Brian Sibley, with art (new and reprinted) by Pauline Baynes; $19.89, 96 pages, Harper & Row Junior Books. Well known for his books on famous fantasy writers such as Tolkien and others, Sibley has written an excellent book for young readers about Lewis, providing background information on Lewis and the writing of the Narnian Chronicles. This book is wonderfully enhanced with Pauline Baynes's delightful and timeless art, many in full color: her map of Narnia, spot illustrations, and full-page illustrations in color and in black and white. With rare photos—Lewis's hand-drawn map of Narnia, a photo of Pauline Baynes in her early twenties when she met Lewis, and more—this book is, in terms of text and art, a reader's joy.

13. *The Pocket Companion to Narnia* by Paul F. Ford; $9.95, trade paperback, 368 pages, HarperSanFrancisco. This is a smaller-sized book, designed for portable use. Measuring four by six inches, this inch-thick book is a condensation of the text from the original book. Highly recommended.

14. *The Quotable Lewis: An Encyclopedic Selection of Quotes from the Complete Published Works of C. S. Lewis*, eds. Wayne Martindale and Jerry Root; $22.99, hardback, 651 pages, Tyndale House Publishers. Arranged alphabetically, this definitive collection is a good way to get an overview of Lewis's thoughts on a wide range of subjects. For adults.

15. *Tolkien and C. S. Lewis: The Gift of Friendship* by Colin Duriez; $16, trade paperback, 244 pages, Paulist Press: HiddenSpring. Intellectual equals and creative giants that conversed, consulted, and sometimes collided with each other, Lewis and Tolkien enjoyed a rare friendship. Born six years apart, the two had more in common than not. Fellow Inklings, college professors, and prolific writers of fiction and nonfiction, Lewis and Tolkien were kindred spirits.

After Lewis's death, Tolkien paid tribute to the importance of Lewis in his life, affirming that without his constant encouragement, *The Lord of the Rings* might never have been completed: "But for his interest and unceasing eagerness for more I should never have brought The L. of the R. to a conclusion. . . ." Highly recommended.

16. *Touring C. S. Lewis' Ireland & England: A Travel Guide to C. S. Lewis' Favorite Places to Walk and Visit* by Perry C. Bramlett and Ronald W. Higdon, with maps by Claudia Wells; $12, trade paperback, 120 pages, Smyth & Helwys Publishing. An informative book that covers places of interest (Ireland, Oxford, Cambridge, and England) in Lewis's personal and professional

life, this is a useful guide, although the maps, located in the rear of the book, make it challenging to use in the field. There's a lot of good information, with detailed entries, but I would prefer to see a layout that integrates the text with the maps in a more useful format, as is found in general guidebooks and access guides.

WEB SITES

The Chronicles of Narnia Website (http://members.lycos.co.uk/ Jonathan_Gregory76/), by Jonathan Gregory. A member of the Children's Literature Ring, this simply designed Web site is rich in information and has a distinct, and wholly appropriate, British orientation, since its author is from the U.K. Devoted exclusively to the Chronicles of Narnia, this is a good place to begin your research about the world beyond the wardrobe.

C. S. Lewis (www.cslewis.com). The official Web site of HarperCollins, which publishes his work worldwide. The Web site includes information about Lewis and his books, reading group guides, a discussion board, and news (through a sign-up e-mail newsletter). Functional and informative, the site's coverage curiously excludes any discussions of the fiction.

C. S. Lewis Foundation: Living the Legacy (www.cslewis.org). A professional Web site devoted to "enabling a genuine renaissance of Christian scholarship and artistic expression within the mainstream of the contemporary university," according to its president, Dr. J. Stanley Mattson. Sponsoring programs and conferences, this foundation offers much to serious students and scholars who share Lewis's worldview and want to immerse themselves in academic scholarship. The foundation also sponsored Oxbridge 2005 (July 24–August 6, 2005), a conference with speakers from the arts, humanities, sciences, and social sciences. (For those unable to attend, an online experience is available, in partnership with the University Centre at http://csl. theucnet.org/cslewis/index.html.)

Hollywood Jesus: Pop Culture from a Spiritual Point of View (www.hollywoodjesus.com), by Greg Wright and Jenn Wright.

A Web site that covers movies, television, comics, books, and music of interest to fellow Christians. Exceptionally thorough and well written.

Into the Wardrobe (www.cslewis.drzeus.net), by John Visser. Recommended by the BBC, this Web site is endorsed by Douglas Gresham, the stepson of C. S. Lewis. Writes Gresham, "Welcome to 'Into the Wardrobe!' I am delighted to have been asked by John Visser, the creator of this excellent web site, to write a few words of introduction. For those who have no idea about Lewis and his work and are just looking for a fun site, there is plenty to investigate and enjoy right here, and what you find here may well lead you into years of enjoyable reading as you discover the existence of one of the finest writers of this century and his books. On the other hand, for those who are already fascinated by Jack (C. S. Lewis's nickname) and his 'Narnian Chronicles' or other works and want to know more about him and his world, you can almost be there yourself by wandering through this site's various links. There is much here of worth to the serious scholar, too, and if you are to embark on a paper about Jack or his works, I heartily recommend this site as a research source. . . . I hope you enjoy your time inside this very large wardrobe." Bookmark this site.

Narnia (www.narnia.com), by Disney Online. Wow. This is one of the most enchanting Web sites I've ever seen. Disney has done a spectacular job with this presentation; no movie has ever had such red-carpet treatment in its promotion. After visiting this site, you will want to see the movie. Bookmark this site!

Narnia Fans (www.narniafans.com). "The goal of 'Narnia Fans' is to deliver the latest news about the film." Run by Christians. Lots of movie news and information about books and Lewis, with a fan section and games as well.

Narniaweb: The World's #1 Source for Narnia Movie News (www. narniaweb.com), by various fans (who go by their screen names only). Founded in November 2003 by Tirian, this is the Narnia fan's equivalent of the Tolkien-centered site The One Ring (www.theonering.net). Covering only the movies, this site is authoritative and exhaustive. "Narniaweb is proud to provide the most comprehensive and accurate information about the new Narnia films being produced by Walden Media. We have a worldwide network of film and media connections (and lots of spies) stretching from America to Europe and all the way to New Zealand. The Narniaweb Discussion Forum hosts a thriving community of Narnia lovers eager to lap up every little detail about the upcoming films." Bookmark this one.

Seminars-in-Residence (www.cslewis.org/programs/kilns/2005). Sponsored by the C. S. Lewis Foundation, this site describes residency programs for students who want not only to immerse themselves in Lewis's texts but also to stay at Lewis's personal residence, lovingly restored to its former beauty—The Kilns, built in 1922 and purchased in 1930 by C. S. Lewis, his brother Warren Lewis, and Mrs. Janie King Moore.

The Stone Table for C. S. Lewis Fans (www.thestonetable.com), by Jamie, Jonathan, and Paul R. Miller. A fan Web site, this is very professional and offers information divided into three categories: the movies, the books, and the man (C. S. Lewis). An e-mailed newsletter is also available.

Virtual Narnia (www.virtualnarnia.com), by Kristi Simonson. A fan Web site, this one will be especially interesting to children, since it covers the art of Narnia, decorating, fan fiction, online games, ideas for student papers, and movie-related links.

Weta Workshop (www.wetaworkshop.co.nz). After teaming up with Sideshow Collectibles to produce a line of acclaimed busts, medallions, statues, and environments from Peter Jackson's film adaptation of *The Lord of the Rings*, Weta Workshop has begun a similar line of collectible sculptures for *The Lion, the Witch and the Wardrobe* to be distributed by Dark Horse. Co-owned by Richard Taylor (company director), Tania Rodger, Peter Jackson, and Jamie Selkirk, Weta is located in Wellington, New Zealand.

Alt.books.cs-lewis is the Usenet discussion group that covers Lewis. (Two related discussion groups: alt.books.inklings and alt.fan.tolkien.rec.arts.books.tolkien.)

What "inspires" my books? Really I don't know. Does anyone know where exactly an idea comes from? With me all fiction begins with pictures in my head.

❖ C. S. Lewis in a 1960 letter to Meredith,
written seven months before his death.

MAP OF NARNIA BY TIM KIRK

CALORMEN

GALMA

TEREBINTHIA

SEVEN ISLES,
LONE
ISLANDS,
ETC.

T. KIRK

ACKNOWLEDGEMENTS

I wish to thank the crew on this voyage to Narnia, the folks at Hampton Roads Publishing who understand the need for "all hands on deck" when a project like this hits the deck. There's no rest for the weary until the ship has made its way to safe harbor, and now that it's done so, let me read the roll call of honor: Robert Friedman, Jack Jennings, Sarah Hilfer, Tania Seymour, Eve Cockrill, Ginna Colburn, Sara Sgarlat, Jane Hagaman, Frank DeMarco, Matthew Genson, and Linda Huffaker.

Thanks, too, to my friends at Weta Workshop and to Laura Schmidt (Archivist, at the Marion E. Wade Center of Wheaton College). Their assistance in securing photos was invaluable.

I owe special thanks to Tim Kirk, who, for the third time, took time out of his busy schedule to help me by providing art for one of my book projects at Hampton Roads Publishing. When it comes to art, he can draw rings around most other artists, and I'm proud to have his work in this book.

For technical assistance, I owe thanks to Ned Brooks, who provided scans of artwork and whose knowledge of fantasy fiction is unsurpassed.

And, finally, I owe my gratitude to Colleen Doran, whose friendship I treasure, and to my wife, Mary, who is a treasure.

Thank you, one and all.

ABOUT
THE AUTHOR
& CONTRIBUTORS

GEORGE BEAHM is the author of several fantasy-related books, including *The J. R. R. Tolkien Sourcebook, Muggles and Magic: An Unofficial Guide to J. K. Rowling and the Harry Potter Phenomenon*, and *Fact, Fiction and Folklore in Harry Potter's World: An Unofficial Guide*. His websites are www.GeorgeBeahm.com and www.FlightsofImagination.com.

TIM KIRK is a design director for Kirk Design, which draws on his vast experience in conceptualization, content creation, and art direction at Walt Disney Imagineering, where he worked for 22 years. Among his many credits at Disney, Kirk was the overall senior designer for Tokyo DisneySea, a $3 billion theme park, and he also played a key role in conceptualizing the popular Disney MGM Studio Tour Park in Walt Disney World. A five-time Hugo award winner for best art in the fantasy and science fiction field, Kirk has illustrated fanzines, calendars, limited edition books, and trade books for numerous publishers. Kirk Design's website is www.kirkdesign.com.

NEIL GAIMAN is the creator/writer of *Sandman*, a comic book series published by D. C. Comics. A bestselling novelist whose novels include *Coraline, American Gods, Anansi Boys, The Wolves in the Walls*, Gaiman's website can be found at www.neilgaiman.com.

Look
for these other companion guides from George Beahm

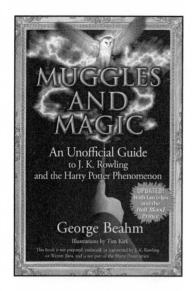

Muggles and Magic: An Unofficial Guide to J. K. Rowling and the Harry Potter Phenomenon. Paperback, 400 pages, $16.95. Featuring more than 60 illustrations and photos. Illustrated by Tim Kirk and Britton McDaniel. With a 16-page full color photo insert.

The first general interest book, resource guide, and reference work on all things Harry Potter, this updated and revised edition is a must for any Potter fan.

Beahm pitches the prose just right; it's both sophisticated enough to interest adults and lively enough to keep younger fans engaged.
   ❖ *Publishers Weekly*

Fact, Fiction, and Folklore in Harry Potter's World: An Unofficial Guide. Paperback, 280 pages, $16.95. With more than 300 alphabetical entries about the beasts, wizards, magical artifacts and enchanting places in Harry Potter's world, this timely tome tells the story behind the world myths, legends, literature, and history in Harry Potter's magical world.

Magicians and muggles alike will benefit from the author's strong attention to detail and interesting descriptions of all things Harry.... A tremendous amount of backstory gives readers new to the series a taste of the first five adventures, whereas seasoned adventurers will rediscover how things magical and muggle have affected Hogwarts' students. Reading this latest guide to the Harry Potter series is like being in class at Hogwarts. The depth and breadth of topics is impressive.
   ❖ *VOYA* (Voice of Youth Advocates)

INDEX

Why is [C. S. Lewis] so popular? . . . Lewis's vivid and luminous imagination is certainly one. His was an imagination not only of invention—with the creation of such worlds as Malacandra, Perelandra, Narnia and Glome. It reveals what in his Preface to *George Mac-Donald: An Anthology* (1847) he called the "divine, magical, terrifying, and ecstatic reality" of the world we actually live in. Lewis's writings are also graced with a clarity that almost takes your breath away. This, in combination with his powerful reason, makes it possible for his works on Christianity to be understood by nearly everyone, including some who are not easily convinced. We could mention as well Lewis's moral toughness, his charity, his love of God, and a wisdom which made him willing to be happy on God's terms.

❖Walter Hooper, *Preface to C. S. Lewis:*
A Complete Guide to His Life & Works

HAMPTON ROADS PUBLISHING COMPANY

. . . for the evolving human spirit

HAMPTON ROADS PUBLISHING COMPANY publishes books
on a variety of subjects, including metaphysics, spirituality,
health, visionary fiction, and other related topics.

For a copy of our latest trade catalog, call toll-free,
800-766-8009, or send your name and address to:

HAMPTON ROADS PUBLISHING COMPANY, INC.
1125 STONEY RIDGE ROAD ● CHARLOTTESVILLE, VA 22902
e-mail: hrpc@hrpub.com ● www.hrpub.com